# MUFFIN COOKBOOK

## 60 QUICK AND EASY RECIPES FOR ANYONE

### SARAH MILLER

# CONTENTS

# INTRODUCTION

There are always some moments when you are hungry, but you don't have enough time to sit and enjoy a complete meal. Sometimes, there is also a situation when you need to bring on-the-go food because you are going mobile without any possibilities to stop by at the restaurants. When those situations happen, a muffin that usually appears in a domed top and a cracked surface can be a perfect solution.

Many people said that muffin is a perfect choice for breakfast. However, the truth is that it is good for any occasion. Coming in many variants of flavor, muffins meet many people's appetites, from kids who love sweet to the old people who usually like something less sweet or savory. They are also perfect for vegetarians because they also can be made without any animal protein. It is obvious; muffin is a suitable choice of food for any age and any situation.

Though muffins are accepted to be delicious and practical food, some people doubt the nutritious content in a cup of muffin since it has a bad reputation of being high in sugar, fats, and carbs. In short, it is considered as high in calories. Well, we cannot say a lot about the store-bought muffins because what is contained in them is a factory's secret.

However, the story will be different from the homemade muffins. For sure, you can control not only the ingredients used in your muffins but also the amount of each of them. Not to mention the baking process as well as the packaging, the storage, and the reheating process. That is why homemade muffins are always better than retail ones.

This book provides 60 recipes that will satisfy your craving at any mealtimes. Of course, those various muffin recipes are also meant to give you as many options as possible in serving a great taste of muffin for your beloved ones, who probably have different favorite flavors. However, before you jump to the recipes, first, you will go to a short explanation of the muffin ingredients, baking process, as well as tips and tricks for successful muffins.

Keep reading and enjoying muffins!

# APPETIZING MUFFINS: HOW TO BAKE, STORE, AND REHEAT

## How to Bake Delicious Muffins

**M**uffins are made in very simple steps. The idea of the muffin cooking process is to blend the dry ingredients mix with the wet mixture, to generate a smooth muffin batter. To make the process clearer, below are the steps by steps of baking muffins that you can follow. Don't worry; this cooking method works for all muffin recipes.

### 1. Combining all dry ingredients

The first step in making muffins is adding all the dry ingredients to a bowl then blend them all. The dry ingredients that are usually used to make muffins could be flour, sweeteners, milk powder, cocoa powder, baking powder, salt, spices, and other ingredients that come in a flour form. As floured ingredients may have lumps, sifting the dry mixture is an unavoidable necessity to generate a very fine texture.

Besides, it is a good way to result in a light and smooth batter.

### 2. Combining all wet ingredients

The second step in the muffin cooking process is mixing the wet ingredients in a separate bowl. The common wet ingredients for muffins are eggs, liquid fats--such as melted butter or oil, cream, milk, vanilla extract, and many more. If you are using some sticky wet ingredients, use a spatula to ensure that everything is completely scraped out from the measuring spoons or cups. Some recipes require combining the sweeteners with the wet ingredients and whisk them until dissolved.

### 3. Mixing the wet mixture with the dry mixture

The next step in the muffin cooking process is mixing the wet mixture with the dry mixture. At this step, you need to pour the wet mixture into the dry mixture and gently fold it until combined. Don't worry if there are a few lumps because it is normal for muffins. For this process, you can use a whisker, a spatula, or anything that you feel comfortable. However, the use of an electric mixer is not recommended because it may result in a tough texture. Usually, some yummy treats like chocolate chips, blueberries, or nuts are added in this step.

### 4. Dividing the batter into muffin tins

When you are done with the batter, take an ice cream scoop and divide the batter into the prepared muffin tins. If you want to add filling or topping, you can do it at this step.

### 5. Baking the muffins

The last step in the muffin making process is baking. It is suggested to bake the muffins between 375°F to 450°F for 20 to 30 minutes, depending on the sizes of the muffins. Preheat the oven until it certainly reaches the desired temperature and bake the muffins until they are light golden brown. However, this does not work on the brown or chocolate muffins since they don't change color as much as the yellow ones. Another way to know if the muffins are done is by inserting a toothpick deeply into the muffins. If the toothpick comes out fully clean, it means the muffins are ready to remove from the oven. Transfer the muffins to a cooling rack and let them cool for a few minutes before serving.

Those are the basic steps by steps in making delicious muffins. Some recipes may require some variation or combination methods based on the ingredients and the expected results. However, all those modified methods are created from the basic one.

## How to Store Muffins in Healthy Ways

After baking a batch or more of delicious muffins, the next thing you have to pay attention to is how to store them. This is necessary because you are likely not going to consume all of the muffins at once. Besides, muffins are also great for any mealtimes, especially when you are busy. That is why; having enough inventories of tasty muffins is beneficial. Other than that, by making the muffins in double batch or more, you will save your time, energy, and money.

The most challenging point in storing the muffins is to keep the muffins moist and soft without getting mushy and stale. For that reason, what you need is a trusted storing technique that will keep your muffins stay fresh and taste as good as the freshly baked ones for the length of time you want to keep the muffins. Below are some ways to store the muffins that you can do.

### 1. Overnight - at room temperature

Since muffins start to dry once they are taken out of the oven, it is not suggested to keep the muffins stay uncovered even for only one night. So, if you bake the muffins the night before and plan to serve them on the next day, it is suggested for you to arrange the muffins on a cooling rack and cover them with a clean tea towel. To make it perfect, you can also put another clean tea towel under the cooling rack. This is a perfect way to keep your muffins tasty yummy fresh.

### 2. Up to 3 Days - in a container with a lid

To keep muffins stay longer, you would better to store them in a container with a lid in a single layer. To avoid the muffins getting soggy, it is recommended to line the container with a paper towel and place another layer of the paper towel over the muffins as well. You don't need to put the container in a refrigerator. However, to keep the muffins stay fresh, you have to ensure that you use an airtight container. This also works for a zipper-lock plastic bag.

### 3. Up to 3 Months - in a freezer

If you want your muffins to last longer, the best you can do is keeping them in the freezer. To freeze the muffins, you can simply arrange them in a zipper-lock plastic bag or an airtight container on a single layer, then freeze them. However, you actually have to remember that you cannot take them in and out many times. For that reason, it is recommended to wrap every single muffin with a sheet of aluminum foil before putting them into the freezer. This will help you to take only the needed portion of the muffins. The muffins will stay up to 3 months in the freezer.

To maximize this storing muffin method, it is highly recommended to label the muffin packages with the date when the muffins were frozen and what flavor they are. This is important to ensure that the muffins will be consumed at the right time. Besides, it helps you to easily find the right flavor, as you desire.

It is your turn to determine how long you want to keep your muffins. However, it is very important to note that for any storing methods you use, the muffins you are going to store have to be completely cooled before storing them. This is needed to keep the muffins from being soggy. Once the muffins are out of the oven, you can arrange them on a cooling rack and let them cool completely. Besides, this will also give time to the muffins to set, so that they will stay in their shapes.

## How to Reheat Muffins When You Need Them

Again, having enough inventories of frozen muffins will feel you like a superhero because you will be able to serve the warm and appetizing muffins in a few minutes. Once you have thawed the muffins at room temperature, reheat them in a microwave for 30 to 40 seconds on High. Besides, you can also re-bake the muffins at 350°F for 10 to 15 minutes. Enjoy!

# APPETIZING MUFFINS: THE INGREDIENTS

You surely have seen so many packages of muffin mixes with an appetizing look of muffin pictures displayed on the front. Sometimes, when you make the muffins, the end products often look nothing like the presented pictures. The worst case is that the muffin mixes often come with pretty yet mysterious names that don't give you any clues of the muffins you are going to make. So, why should you bother yourself with all of the mystery?

Muffin is a baked product that is easy to prepare from scratch. The basic ingredients like flour, sweeteners, eggs, and fats are very easy to find, and the additional ingredients can follow your creativity. To help you mix and match the ingredients to make your delicious muffins, below are some options for both basic and additional ingredients.

**Flours**

Multi-purpose flour, whole grain flour, almond flour, coconut flour

**Sweeteners**

Granulated sugar, powdered sugar, brown sugar

**Eggs**

Pastured eggs, organic eggs

**Liquids**

Plain yogurt, fresh milk, sour cream, heavy cream

**Fats**

Butter, margarine, applesauce, olive oil, sunflower oil, canola oil, vegetable oil

**Nuts**

Walnuts, peanuts, almonds, pecan

**Chocolates**

Choco chips, cocoa powder, dark chocolate compound, chocolate sprinkles

**Leavening**

Baking soda, baking powder

**Flavors & Spices**

The ground cinnamon, cardamom, cloves, ginger, allspices, vanilla extract, vanilla

**Others**

Oatmeal

**Fruits**

Blueberries, cranberries, strawberries, apples, pineapples, oranges, lemons, dried raisins,

## APPETIZING MUFFINS: THE BASIC TOOLS

**M**any may say that baking needs complicated equipment, like what we have seen in the bakery. That may be true. However, muffin baking is an exception. You can bake tasty muffins with minimal equipment. Even you can always maximize all your kitchen tools as long as they have the same function.

Below is the list of basic equipment needed in baking muffins.

- Mixing bowls
- Measuring cups
- Measuring spoons
- A sifter
- A whisk
- A spatula
- A soup ladle or an ice cream scoop
- Muffin tins
- An oven

• A cooling rack

Those are some basic equipment that you need to bake muffins. Other equipment, such as a cheese grater, a knife, a spatula, a skewer, a timer, an oven mitt, a blender, or a food processor that may be needed in baking your delicious muffins, are usually available in the kitchen. For sure, you can simply use them and no need to buy the new ones. However, if they are not available in your kitchen and you have no opportunity to buy them, you can use other tools that you can find, or you can also modify the recipes so that you don't have to use those tools. For example: if a cheese grater is not available, you can cut the cheese into very small cubes so that you don't need to shred it.

# APPETIZING MUFFINS: TIPS AND TRICKS FOR SUCCESSFUL MUFFINS

A s mentioned above, baking muffins does not require a specific baking skill. However, to generate the perfect muffins, there are some tips and tricks that you can follow.

• Always measure the ingredients carefully. If it is necessary, level the ingredients in measuring spoons to get an exact amount of the ingredients.

• Always check the expired date of the ingredients to make sure that your ingredients are still in the best condition.

• Fresh leavening agents help to rise and give a perfect texture of the muffins.

• Do not over stir the muffin batter because it will make the muffin bake unevenly and create peaked tops to the muffin.

• Line the muffin tins with paper liners. If paper liners

are not available, make sure to grease the muffin tins with melted butter or oil spray.

• Coating the fruits for topping or filling with flour will help to avoid them sinking to the bottom of the muffins.

• Frozen fruits, such as frozen blueberries may streak the color of the muffin batter.

• A small cookie scoop or a soup ladle will help you to transfer the muffin batter to the prepared muffin tins without making a mess.

• Fill your muffin tins with the batter about ¾ full to prevent the batter from spilling out over the tins.

• Always preheat the oven before inserting the muffins into it.

• If you actually don't have enough batter to fill the entire muffin tins, you should fill the empty tins with water to keep the muffin pan from warping.

• If you get difficulties in taking the muffins out of the tins, you can place the muffin tins on a wet towel for a few minutes. It will help to release the muffins from the tins.

So, now you have already known about the keys to successful muffins. There is nothing to wait for. Grab your favorite muffin recipes below and start baking yours.

Happy baking!

# MUFFINS RECIPES

## Triple Chocolate Moist Muffins

This muffin can be considered as a nice collaboration between brownies and cakes. It has a fudgy and moist texture inside but also offers a crispy sensation on top. The chocolate sprinkles on top truly give another classic chocolate taste to your muffin. Make sure to use only good quality of chocolate sprinkles to satisfy your tongue.

**Yield:** 10-12 mini muffins

**Cooking time:** 30 minutes

**Ingredients:**

- ½ cup multi-purpose flour
- ¾ cup granulated sugar
- ¼ cup cocoa powder
- ¼ teaspoon salt
- ¾ teaspoon baking soda
- 2 eggs
- 1 teaspoon vanilla extract
- ⅓ cup plain yogurt
- ¼ cup salted butter
- ¼ cup margarine
- ½ cup chopped dark chocolate compound

**Topping:**

- ¾ cup chocolate sprinkles

**Instructions:**

1. First, preheat an oven to 425°F (218°C) and prepare 12 mini muffin tins. Put a paper cup into each muffin tin then set aside.

2. Melt the dark chocolate compound together with butter and margarine then let it cool.

3. Next, combine the multi-purpose flour with cocoa powder, baking soda, and salt then mix well. Set aside.

4. In a separate bowl, place vanilla extract, sugar, eggs, plain yogurt, and the melted butter mixture then whisk the ingredients until incorporated.

5. Pour the wet mixture into the dry mixture then fold it until combined. Make sure that there is no flour at the bottom and the side of the bowl that has not been mixed.

6. Next, using a soup ladle or an ice cream spoon the

muffin batter to the prepared muffin tins then sprinkle chocolate sprinkles on top.

7. Insert the muffins to the oven and bake them for 15 to 18 minutes or until a toothpick or a small stick inserted to the muffins comes out clean.

8. Once it is done, remove the muffins from the oven and let them cool in the muffin tins for approximately 5 minutes.

9. Carefully take the muffins out of the muffin tins and transfer them to a cooling rack.

10. Serve and enjoy.

**Choco Lava Muffins**

It is like happiness that suddenly comes to you on the first bite. Melted on your tongue, the chocolate lava that flows from inside of these muffins tastes so rich that it will make your tongue dances. Since the inside of the muffins will always be wet, you can check the doneness of the muffins by looking at the edges and the center of the muffins. Once the edges are well cooked all around, and the center has risen and looks firm, that means that the muffins are done.

**Yield:** 10-12 muffins

**Cooking time:** 18 minutes

**Ingredients:**
- 1 cup chocolate chips
- ¾ cup granulated sugar
- ¾ cup butter
- 1 teaspoon vanilla extract
- 3 eggs
- 3 egg yolks
- ¼ cup multi-purpose flour

**Instructions:**

1. Melt the butter together with the chocolate chips in a microwave then let it cool for a few minutes.

2. Preheat an oven to 350°F (177°C) and prepare 12 muffin tins. Line each muffin cup with a paper cup and set aside.

3. Next, add sugar, vanilla extract, egg yolks, and whole eggs to the melted butter then stir until incorporated.

4. Stir in the multi-purpose flour to the wet mixture then mix well.

5. Carefully divide the batter into the prepared muffin tins then bake them for 8 to 10 minutes or until the edges of the muffins are set. The center of the muffins will be soft.

6. Once it is done, remove the muffins from the oven and let them cool for 2 minutes.

7. Serve and enjoy.

## Cocoa Muffins with Coconut Sweet Topping

This muffin can be another option for chocolate muffin lovers. The coconut topping in this muffin tastes sweet because it is mixed with brown sugar. However, if you like it to be savory, you can simply remove the brown sugar and just combine the grated coconut with the evaporated milk. To make it a little aromatic, you can add nutmeg, cinnamon, and salt to the coconut topping mixture.

**Yield:** 10-12 muffins

**Cooking time:** 20 minutes

**Ingredients:**

- 1½ cups multi-purpose flour
- 5 tablespoons unsweetened cocoa powder
- ¼ teaspoon salt
- 1 teaspoon baking soda
- 1 teaspoon baking powder
- ½ cup granulated sugar
- 2 tablespoons brown sugar
- ¾ cup sour cream
- ¼ cup fresh milk
- 2 eggs
- 1 teaspoon vanilla extract

• ¼ cup unsalted butter

**Topping:**

• ¼ cup brown sugar

• ¼ cup grated coconut

• 2 tablespoons evaporated milk

**Instructions:**

1. Melt butter over low heat then let it cool for a few minutes.

2. Preheat an oven to 325°F (191°C) and line 12 muffin tins with paper cups. Set aside.

3. Mix the multi-purpose flour with cocoa powder, baking soda, baking powder, and salt then stir until combined.

4. Mix granulated sugar with brown sugar in a mixing bowl then add sour cream, fresh milk, eggs, and vanilla extract. Whisk until incorporated.

5. After that, pour the melted butter into the wet mixture then stir well.

6. Next, mix the wet mixture with the dry mixture then fold it until smooth and creamy.

7. Carefully divide the mixture into the prepared muffin tins then set aside.

8. Add the brown sugar to the grated coconut then pour evaporated milk into the mixture. Using your fingers mix until combined.

9. Sprinkle the coconut mixture on top of the muffins then bake them for 20 minutes.

10. Once the muffins are done, carefully move them from the oven and let them rest in the tins for 5 minutes.

11. Transfer the muffins on a cooling rack. Then, let them cool.

12. Serve and enjoy.

## Chocolate Brownie Muffins

Just like a brownie, this muffin comes with a firm but moist texture. The dark chocolate compound that is used in this recipe also surely takes a role in giving an extra chocolate flavor for the brownie muffin. However, if you like the texture of the muffin but want to try any other taste besides chocolate, you can replace the dark chocolate compound with the white one. To make it completely perfect, you also need to remove the cocoa powder and substitute it with multi-purpose flour and cornstarch. The amount of cornstarch should not be more than 20% of the amount of multi-purpose flour. Don't forget to add flavor, as you desired.

**Yield:** 10-12 muffins

**Cooking time:** 20 minutes

**Ingredients:**

- ½ cup butter
- ¾ cup chopped dark chocolate compound
- ½ cup brown sugar
- ¼ cup granulated sugar

- 1 teaspoon baking soda
- 1 teaspoon vanilla extract
- 2 eggs
- ¾ cup plain yogurt
- ¼ teaspoon salt
- 1½ cups multi-purpose flour
- ½ cup unsweetened cocoa powder

**Instructions:**

1. Melt butter together with chopped dark chocolate compound, brown sugar, and granulated sugar then let it cool for a few minutes.

2. Next, preheat an oven to 425°F (218°C) and line 12 muffin tins with paper cups. Set aside.

3. Crack the eggs and place them in a mixing bowl.

4. Add plain yogurt and vanilla extract to the melted butter mixture then stir until incorporated.

5. Pour the yogurt and egg mixture into the melted butter then mix well.

6. After that, combine multi-purpose flour with baking soda, salt, and cocoa powder then sift them.

7. Next, gradually, add the dry mixture to the wet mixture then whisk until combined.

8. Using a soup ladle divide the batter into the prepared muffin tins then bakes them.

9. Once the muffins are done, remove them from the oven and let them rest in the muffins tins. Transfer them to a cooling rack.

10. Serve and enjoy.

## Nutella Cocoa Brownies with Buttermilk

This is a fabulous muffin that you never want to stop eating it. For sure, who doesn't like Nutella? The hazelnut content in Nutella surely boosts your heart health, while the chocolate taste satisfies your appetite. For an extraordinary delicacy and appearance, you can add a swirl of Nutella on top of each muffin. There is no doubt; the muffin will be very special.

**Yield:** 10-12 muffins

**Cooking time:** 20 minutes

**Ingredients:**
- 1½ cups multi-purpose flour
- ½ cup unsweetened cocoa powder
- ½ teaspoon baking soda
- 1 teaspoon baking powder
- A pinch of salt
- 1 cup brown sugar
- 1 egg
- 1½ cups buttermilk
- 2 tablespoons butter
- ¾ cup Nutella
- ¼ cup chocolate chunks

**Instructions:**

1. Melt butter over low heat then let it cool. Set aside.

2. Preheat an oven to 400°F (204°C) and line 12 muffin tins with paper cups. Set aside.

3. Combine the multi-purpose flour with cocoa powder, baking powder, baking soda, and salt then mix well.

4. In another bowl, whisk the brown sugar with egg then add buttermilk and melted butter to the mixture. Stir until incorporated.

5. Next, mix the wet mixture with the dry mixture then fold to combine.

6. Drop a tablespoon of batter into each prepared muffin cup.

7. Add a tablespoon of Nutella on top of the batter then cover the Nutella with the remaining batter.

8. Sprinkle chocolate chunks on top then bake the muffins in the preheated oven.

9. Once it is done, remove the muffins from the oven and let them rest in the muffin tins for 5 minutes.

10. Take the muffins out of the muffins tins then arrange them on a cooling rack.

11. Serve and enjoy.

# Coconut Sugar Chocolate Muffins with Oat Flour

Coconut sugar is considered as one of the healthy sugar alternatives. Comparing with other kinds of sugar, the coconut sugar is more nutritious and has a lower glycemic index for it is made from a coconut palm tree. Besides, this muffin also uses oat flour that is rich in dietary fiber, protein, and healthy fats. Therefore, the muffin has become a great choice for you who always put health as a priority. If oat flour is not available, you can easily grind regular oat until becoming flour texture.

**Yield:** 10-12 muffins

**Cooking time:** 20 minutes

**Ingredients:**

- ¾ cup unsweetened cocoa powder
- 1½ cups oat flour
- ½ cup coconut sugar
- ¼ teaspoon salt
- 1 teaspoon baking powder
- 1 cup unsweetened almond milk
- ¾ cup unsweetened applesauce
- 6 tablespoons butter
- 1 teaspoon vanilla extract

• 2 tablespoons apple cider vinegar

**Instructions:**

1. Melt butter over low heat then let it cool. Set aside.

2. Preheat an oven to 360°F (182°C) and line 12 muffin tins with paper cups. Set aside.

3. Combine the oat flour with coconut sugar, cocoa powder, baking powder, and salt then mix well.

4. In another bowl, whisk the almond milk, applesauce, melted butter, applesauce, and vanilla extract then stir until incorporated.

5. Next, gradually pour the wet mixture into the dry mixture then fold until combined.

6. Using an ice cream scoop divide the batter into the prepared muffin tins then insert them into the preheated oven and bake the muffins.

7. Bake the muffins for 25-28 minutes and check the muffins. Once a toothpick inserted into the muffins comes out clean, carefully remove the muffins from the oven.

8. Then, let the muffins rest in the tins for 5 minutes. Take them out of the tins and transfer them to a cooling rack.

9. Serve and enjoy.

# Black Oreo Mocha Muffins

If you are an Oreo lover, and you want to involve the rich taste of Oreo into your muffin, this recipe surely fits you. Using brewed coffee and milk as the source of liquid ingredients, this muffin offers a flavorsome taste that is resulted from the combination of Oreo, coffee, and chocolate. For this unique taste, it is suggested that you not to replace the ingredients or change the measurement.

**Yield:** 10-12 muffins

**Cooking time:** 35 minutes

**Ingredients:**

- 1 cup multi-purpose flour
- ½ cup unsweetened cocoa powder
- 1 egg
- ¼ teaspoon salt
- 1 teaspoon vanilla extract
- ½ teaspoon baking soda
- 1 teaspoon baking powder
- 1 cup granulated sugar
- ½ cup fresh milk
- ¼ cup corn oil

- ½ cup brewed coffee
- 15 pieces Oreo

**Instructions:**

1. Discard the cream inside the Oreos then place the Oreos in a food processor. Process until becoming crumbles and set aside.

2. Next, preheat an oven to 350°F (177°C) and line 12 muffin tins with paper cups. Set aside.

3. Add baking powder, baking soda, cocoa powder, and salt to the multi-purpose flour then stir until combined. Sift the flour.

4. In another bowl, whisk sugar with egg then pour fresh milk, brewed coffee, vanilla extract, and corn oil. Stir until incorporated.

5. Gradually mix the wet mixture with the dry mixture then add the Oreo crumbles to the batter. Fold to combine.

6. Using an ice cream scoop divide the batter into the prepared muffin tins then bakes the muffins.

7. Once it is done, remove the muffins from the oven and let them rest in the muffin tins for 5 minutes.

8. Carefully take the muffins out of the muffin tins then arrange them on a cooling rack.

9. Serve and enjoy.

## No Eggs Banana Muffins

If you have sensitivities to eggs, then this muffin recipe is best for you. Without any presence of eggs, this muffin is a perfect choice for those who have egg-allergic or are in reducing cholesterol level program. Although it is eggless, the texture of the muffin is still moist and tender. The key to the fluffy texture is indeed the usage of baking soda and vinegar. The combination of these two works as a raising agent that gives a perfect look for the muffin.

**Yield:** 10-12 muffins

**Cooking time:** 35 minutes

**Ingredients:**

- ¼ cup vegetable oil
- 1 cup granulated sugar
- 2 cups multi-purpose flour
- 4 ripe bananas
- ¼ teaspoon salt
- 1 teaspoon baking soda
- 1 teaspoon vinegar

**Instructions:**

1. Preheat an oven to 360°F (182°C) and line 12 muffin tins with paper cups. Set aside.

2. Peel the bananas and mash them until smooth.

3. Pour vegetable oil and vinegar into the mashed bananas then stir until incorporated.

4. Add granulated sugar to the wet mixture then mix well. Set aside.

5. Combine the multi-purpose flour with salt and baking soda then mix well.

6. Stir in the dry mixture to the wet mixture then fold until combined.

7. Using an ice cream scoop divide the batter into the prepared muffin tins then inserts them to the preheated oven. Bake the muffins.

8. Once it is done, remove the muffins from the oven then let them rest in the muffin tins for 5 minutes.

9. Transfer the muffins to a cooling rack and let them cool.

10. Serve and enjoy.

## Brownie Milo Banana Muffins

The amazing taste of Milo will attract you from the first bite. For sure, it contributes to the creamy and malty flavor of this muffin that will satisfy your appetite. For the best result, it is suggested not to reduce the amount of Milo in this recipe. Even if you want it to be richer in Milo taste, you can add the amount of Milo into the muffin. However, you should remember that as a consequence, you have to reduce the amount of multi-purpose flour you use for the muffin.

**Yield:** 10-12 muffins

**Cooking time:** 20 minutes

**Ingredients:**

- 1½ cups multi-purpose flour
- 1 teaspoon baking powder
- 3 tablespoons brown sugar
- ½ cup Milo
- ½ cup fresh milk
- 1 egg
- 3 tablespoons butter
- 2 ripe bananas

**Instructions:**

1. Melt the butter over low heat. Then, set aside.

2. After that, peel the bananas then mash them until smooth.

3. Next, preheat an oven to 425°F (218°C) and line 12 muffin tins with paper cups. Set aside.

4. Combine the multi-purpose flour with brown sugar, baking powder, and Milo then mix well.

5. Crack the egg then combine it with the fresh milk. Stir until incorporated.

6. Pour the egg mixture into the flour mixture then mix well.

7. Add melted butter to the mixture then stir until combined.

8. Next, stir in the mashed bananas and using a spatula fold until incorporated.

9. Using an ice cream scoop divide the batter into the prepared muffin tins then inserts them into the preheated oven. Bake the muffins.

10. Once it is done, remove the muffins from the oven and let them rest in the tins for 5 minutes.

11. Transfer the muffins to a cooling rack. Then, let them cool.

12. Serve and enjoy.

## Caramel Crumbles Banana Muffins

A caramel topping is the soul of muffin. It makes a basic muffin look more tempting and taste special. To get the sweet topping without getting it burnt, you have to pay attention to the temperature of these muffins. For the most amazing result, add the baking time for about one minute on upper heat right after the muffins are done.

**Yield:** 10-12 muffins

**Cooking time:** 30 minutes

**Ingredients:**

• 1½ cups multi-purpose flour

- 1 teaspoon baking soda
- ¼ teaspoon salt
- ½ cup olive oil
- ½ cup honey
- ¼ cup plain yogurt
- 1 teaspoon vanilla extract
- 2 eggs
- 4 ripe bananas

**Topping:**
- ¼ cup brown sugar
- ½ teaspoon ground cinnamon
- 3 tablespoons multi-purpose flour
- ¼ cup salted butter

**Instructions:**

1. Peel the bananas then mash them until smooth. Set aside.

2. Preheat an oven to 380°F (193°C) and line 12 muffin tins with paper cups. Set aside.

3. Add salt and baking soda to the multi-purpose flour then mix well.

4. In another bowl, combine eggs with honey, olive oil, plain yogurt, and vanilla extract then stir until incorporated.

5. Next, gradually pour the wet mixture into the dry mixture then mix well.

6. Fold in the mashed bananas to the batter then stir until combined.

7. Using an ice cream scoop spoon the batter and drop it into the prepared muffin tins. Set aside.

8. Next, combine brown sugar, cinnamon, and multi-purpose flour in a bowl then mix well.

9. Cut the salted butter into small cubes then add them to the brown sugar mixture. Using your fingers mix the ingredients until becoming crumbles.

10. Sprinkle the brown sugar crumbles over the muffins then bake them for 20 to 22 minutes.

11. Once the muffins are done, remove them from oven and let them cool for 5 minutes in the tins.

12. Carefully take the muffins out of the muffin tins and arrange them on a cooling rack and wait until the muffins are completely cool.

13. Serve and enjoy.

## Banana Pecans Muffins with Date Sugar

There is no doubt that the banana muffin is very famous. It offers a delicious muffin with a soft texture. However, adding some chopped pecans to the banana muffin is a different story. For sure, it gives a crunchy sensation in the mild muffin. Besides, the usage of the date sugar in this muffin recipe is surely a plus. Certainly, it is a type of sugar that is natural and healthy.

**Yield:** 10-12 muffins

**Cooking time:** 35 minutes

**Ingredients:**
- ½ cup date sugar
- 2 cups multi-purpose flour
- 1 teaspoon baking powder
- 1 teaspoon baking soda
- 2 eggs
- 6 ripe bananas
- 1 teaspoon vanilla extract
- ½ cup butter
- ¾ cup chopped pecans
- 1 tablespoon caster sugar
- 1 teaspoon ground cinnamon

**Instructions:**

1. Peel the bananas then mash them until smooth. Set aside.

2. Preheat an oven to 350°F (177°C) and line 12 muffin tins with paper cups. Set aside.

3. Place butter and date sugar in a mixing bowl then using an electric mixer beat it until smooth.

4. Crack the eggs then place them in a bowl.

5. Continue mixing the batter until creamy then add the mashed bananas and vanilla extract to it. Fold it until combined.

6. Next, the multi-purpose flour with baking soda and baking powder then add the mixture to the batter. Mix well.

7. After that, add the chopped pecans to the batter then using a spatula fold them until well combined.

8. Divide the batter into the prepared muffin tins then bake them for 20 to 25 minutes or until a toothpick inserted deeply into the muffins comes out clean.

9. Once it is done, remove the muffins from the oven and let them cool for 5 minutes. Transfer the muffins to a cooling rack.

10. Serve and enjoy.

## Coffee Mocha Banana Marble Muffins

Surprisingly, adding coffee and cocoa to a banana muffin is a great idea. This muffin performs a mixed mocha and banana flavor that comes in every single bite you make. A blunder that may happen in the muffin making is the bitter taste of the coffee powder that is not perfectly dissolved. To avoid this happens in the future, you have to make sure that you use very hot water to dissolve the coffee. For the better result, it is better to strain the brewed coffee before pouring it into the batter.

**Yield:** 10-12 muffins

**Cooking time:** 30 minutes

**Ingredients:**

- 1¼ cups multi-purpose flour
- ¾ cup granulated sugar
- ¼ teaspoon salt
- 1 teaspoon baking powder

- 1 tablespoon instant coffee powder
- 1 tablespoon hot water
- 6 tablespoons softened butter
- 1 egg
- 3 ripe bananas
- 1 tablespoon cocoa powder
- 1 teaspoon vanilla extract

**Instructions:**

1. First, preheat an oven to 350°F (177°C) and prepared 12 muffin tins. Place a paper cup in each muffin tin then set aside.

2. Peel the bananas then mash them until smooth. Set aside.

3. Add coffee powder to the hot water then stir until dissolved. Set aside.

4. After that, combine the multi-purpose flour with baking soda and salt then mix well.

5. Place the butter together with sugar in a mixing bowl then using an electric mixer beat until smooth and creamy.

6. Add egg to the creamy mixture then beat well.

7. Beat in the mashed bananas together with vanilla extract and the coffee mixture then remove the mixer.

8. Stir in the multi-purpose flour mixture then using a spatula fold the batter until combined.

9. Take a quarter of the batter then mix it with the cocoa powder.

10. Next, fill half of the muffin tins with the white batter then drop a tablespoon of cocoa batter on each muffin tins.

11. Cover each muffin with the remaining white batter

then using a toothpick stir the muffins to give a marble texture.

12. Then, insert the muffins into the oven and bake them for 18 to 20 minutes.

13. Once it is done, remove the muffins from the oven and let them cool in the muffin tins for 5 minutes. Transfer the muffins to a cooling rack.

14. Serve and enjoy.

**Banana Flax Muffins with Raisins and Cranberries**

Have you ever tried to replace eggs with flax seed? If you have never done that before, this recipe can be a try. The ground flax seed that is mixed with liquid is a great option of egg replacement in baking. Many people say that ground flax seed is a good option for vegan. In fact, it is good for everyone since ground flax seed is rich in fiber and omega-3 fatty acids.

**Yield:** 10-12 muffins

**Cooking time:** 30 minutes

**Ingredients:**

- 1 cup multi-purpose flour
- ¼ teaspoon salt

- 1 teaspoon ground cinnamon
- 1 teaspoon baking powder
- ¼ cup unsweetened almond milk
- 1 tablespoon ground flax
- 3 tablespoons olive
- 3 tablespoons maple syrup
- 1 teaspoon vanilla extract
- 2 ripe bananas
- 3 tablespoons raisins
- 3 tablespoons chopped cranberries

**Instructions:**

1. Mix the ground flax with almond milk then whisk until incorporated. set aside.

2. Preheat an oven to 350°F (177°C) and prepared 12 muffin tins. Place a paper cup in each muffin tin then set aside.

3. Add baking powder, ground cinnamon, and salt to the multi-purpose flour then mix well.

4. Next, in a separate bowl, combine the olive oil with maple syrup and vanilla extract then stir well.

5. Peel the bananas then mash them until smooth.

6. Add the mashed bananas together with the flax mixture to the wet mixture then stir until incorporated.

7. Stir in the dry mixture to the wet mixture then fold until combined.

8. Add raisins and chopped cranberries to the batter then mix well.

9. Next, divide the batter into the prepared muffin tins. Bake them for approximately 17 to 20 minutes.

10. Once the muffins are done, let them rest in the muffin tins for 5 minutes then transfer them to a cooling rack.

11. Serve and enjoy.

## Banana Oat Muffins with Canola Oil

This is a nutritious muffin that will keep you full for quite a long time. That is why; this muffin is highly recommended for breakfast on a busy morning. The oat content both inside and top of the muffin is high in fiber and protein, which surely give extra satiety to your tummy. The taste and the texture of the muffin will not disappoint you as well since it is made with bananas and canola oil. For sure, those two ingredients take a role in giving moist texture to the muffin.

**Yield:** 10-12 muffins

**Cooking time:** 30 minutes

**Ingredients:**

- 3 ripe bananas
- ½ cup unsweetened almond milk
- ¼ cup canola oil
- 1 teaspoon vanilla extract
- 1 tablespoon apple cider vinegar
- ¼ cup brown sugar
- 1¼ cups multi-purpose flour
- ¼ cup quick-cooking oats
- 1 teaspoon baking powder

- ¾ teaspoon ground cinnamon
- ¼ teaspoon salt

**Topping:**

- 3 tablespoons quick-cooking oats
- 3 tablespoons granulated sugar

**Instructions:**

1. First, preheat an oven to 350°F (177°C) and prepared 12 muffin tins. Place a paper cup in each muffin tin then set aside.

2. Peel the bananas then mash them until smooth.

3. Pour almond milk into the mashed bananas together with canola oil, vanilla extract, and apple cider vinegar then stir until incorporated.

4. In another bowl, combine brown sugar with the multi-purpose flour, quick-cooking oats, baking powder, cinnamon, and salt then mix well.

5. Next, combine the wet mixture with the dry mixture then whisk until incorporated.

6. Using an ice cream scoop divide the batter into the prepared muffin tins then sprinkles the topping mixture on top.

7. Insert the muffins into the preheated oven then bake them.

8. Insert a toothpick into the muffins and once it comes out clean, remove the muffins from the oven and let them rest for 5 minutes.

9. Transfer the muffins to a cooling rack and let them cool.

10. Serve and enjoy.

## Classic Vanilla Muffin Streusels

Just like its name, this vanilla muffin is made based on a classic recipe with sugar, egg, flour, milk, and butter. You will probably not have a big expectation upon first glance, but surprisingly, the result is amazing. Once this muffin goes out of the oven, you will not only get the warm muffin, but more than that, you will enjoy the moist, tender, and light muffin. If you like, you may serve the muffin with vanilla glaze, marmalade, or any kind of fruit preserves.

**Yield:** 10-12 muffins

**Cooking time:** 30 minutes

**Ingredients:**

- ½ cup salted butter
- ¾ cup granulated sugar
- 2 eggs
- 1 teaspoon vanilla extract
- 1½ cups multi-purpose flour
- 1½ teaspoons baking powder
- ½ cup fresh milk

**Topping:**

- ½ cup brown sugar
- ¼ cup granulated sugar

- ½ cup multi-purpose flour
- 2 teaspoons ground cinnamon
- A pinch of salt
- ¼ cup unsalted butter

**Instructions:**

1. Combine the topping mixture in a bowl.

2. Next, cut the butter into small cubes. Then, add brown sugar, granulated sugar, multi-purpose flour, cinnamon, and salt using your fingers mix until becoming crumbles. Set aside.

3. Then, preheat an oven to 400°F (204°C) and prepare 12 muffin tins. Line each muffin tin with a paper cup.

4. Place the butter in a mixing bowl together with the granulated sugar then using an electric mixer beat until smooth and creamy.

5. Add eggs and vanilla extract to butter mixture then beat again until fluffy.

6. Combine the multi-purpose flour with baking powder then add the dry mixture to the butter mixture. Mix well.

7. After that, pour the fresh milk into the mixture then mix until creamy and smooth.

8. Using a spoon divide the batter into the prepared muffin tins then sprinkles the topping on top.

9. Insert the muffins into the oven. Then, bake them.

10. Once the muffins are done, carefully remove them from the oven and let them rest for 5 minutes in the muffin tins.

11. Then, let the muffins cool on a cooling rack and serve.

12. Enjoy.

# Choco Chips Vanilla Muffins with Parsley

Who has ever thought that parsley and vanilla cannot be a good partner? This vanilla muffin proves that they are a great combination. The muffin does not only perform delicious taste but also health benefits. For sure, parsley can prevent cancer, protect diabetes, and improve bone health. For the best result, it is indeed best to use fresh parsley. However, if fresh parsley is not available, dried parsley is still acceptable.

**Yield:** 10-12 muffins

**Cooking time:** 30 minutes

**Ingredients:**

- ¾ cup fresh milk
- 1½ cups multi-purpose flour
- 6 tablespoons plain yogurt
- ¼ cup vegetable oil
- 1 teaspoon vanilla extract
- ½ cup brown sugar
- ¼ teaspoon salt
- 1 teaspoon baking powder
- 2 tablespoons diced parsley
- ½ cup Choco chips

**Instructions:**

1. First, preheat an oven to 350°F (177°C) and prepare 12 muffin tins. Line each muffin cup with a paper cup.

2. Mix the multi-purpose flour with brown sugar, baking powder, diced parsley, and salt. Set aside.

3. In another bowl, combine the fresh milk, plain yogurt, vegetable oil, and vanilla extract then stir until incorporated.

4. Next, gradually pour the wet mixture into the dry mixture then whisk until combined.

5. Add the Choco chips to the batter then fold to mix.

6. Using an ice cream scoop divide the batter into the prepared muffin tins then inserts them into the preheated oven. Bake the muffins.

7. Once it is done, remove the muffins from the oven and let them rest in the muffin tins for 5 minutes.

8. Transfer the muffins to a cooling rack. Serve.

9. Enjoy!


**Cinnamon Sweet Potato Muffins with Coconut Milk**

If you are actually looking for a muffin recipe that is nutritious with less sugar, then this one is definitely yours. The natural sweetness of the sweet potatoes makes this muffin tastes flavorful, while the smooth texture of the mashed sweet potatoes results in a firm but moist texture. In short, the muffin is a complete package of healthy and tasty food.

**Yield:** 10-12 muffins

**Cooking time:** 30 minutes

**Ingredients:**

- 1 cup multi-purpose flour
- 3 tablespoons granulated sugar
- 1 teaspoon baking powder
- ¼ teaspoon salt
- ¾ teaspoon ground cinnamon
- 1 egg
- ½ cup mashed sweet potatoes
- ¼ canola oil

**Instructions:**

1. Preheat an oven to 325°F (191°C) and prepare 12 muffin tins. Line each muffin tin with a paper cup.

2. Combine the multi-purpose flour with sugar, baking powder, salt, and ground cinnamon then mix well.

3. Add mashed sweet potato together with egg, coconut milk, and canola oil then mix until combined.

4. Next, using an ice cream scoop, carefully divide the mixture into the prepared muffin tins then insert them into the preheated oven and bake them.

5. Once it is done, remove the muffins from the oven and take them out of the muffin tins.

6. Let the muffins cool on a cooling rack and serve.

7. Enjoy!

## Yogurt Moist Muffins with Chocolate Chips

Moist, light, and fluffy; those are some words that suit to describe this muffin. This muffin uses yogurt as the main liquid that results in a delicious muffin, just like what has been described in the first sentence. If you like a strong butter taste, it is suggested to use plain yogurt. However, if you like a flavored muffin, you would better use blueberry yogurt, strawberry yogurt, or any other yogurt with extra flavors.

**Yield:** 10-12 muffins

**Cooking time:** 30 minutes

**Ingredients:**

- 1¼ cups multi-purpose flour
- ¼ teaspoon salt
- 1 teaspoon baking powder
- ½ cup granulated sugar
- 1 egg
- ½ cup plain yogurt
- 3 tablespoons butter
- 2 tablespoons fresh milk
- ¼ cup Choco chips

**Instructions:**

1. First, melt the butter over low heat. Then, let it cool and set aside.

2. Second, preheat an oven to 350°F (177°C) and prepare 12 muffin tins. Line each muffin tin with a paper cup.

3. Combine the multi-purpose flour with salt and baking powder then mix well. Sift the dry mixture.

4. In another bowl, whisk the granulated sugar with the egg then pour plain yogurt, fresh milk, and melted butter into it. Stir until incorporated.

5. Next, gradually pour the wet mixture into the dry mixture then fold to combine.

6. Using a soup ladle divide the batter into the prepared muffin tins then sprinkles Choco chips on top.

7. Insert the muffins into the preheated oven then bake them for 20 to 22 minutes or until a toothpick that is inserted into the muffins comes out clean.

8. Once it is done, remove the muffins from the oven and let them rest in the muffin tins for 5 minutes.

9. Take the muffins out of the tins then let them cool on a cooling rack.

10. Serve and enjoy.

## Blueberry Muffin with Olive Oil

There is no doubt that olive oil comes with a bunch of health benefits. It is, for sure, a source of healthy fats and antioxidants that are good for body metabolism. Besides, the olive oil also makes this muffin super moist and will stay moist longer than other muffins, even if it has been left at room temperature. However, for longer shelf life, it is suggested to keep the muffin in the freezer.

**Yield:** 10-12 muffins

**Cooking time:** 30 minutes

**Ingredients:**

- 1½ cups multi-purpose flour
- ½ teaspoon salt
- 1½ teaspoons baking powder
- 2 eggs
- ½ cup granulated sugar
- ½ cup fresh milk
- 1 teaspoon vanilla extract
- ⅓ cup olive oil
- 1 cup fresh blueberries

**Instructions:**

1. First, preheat an oven to 400°F (204°C) and prepare 12

muffin tins. Put a paper cup into each muffin tin and set aside.

2. Combine the multi-purpose flour with salt and baking powder then stir well.

3. Place the sugar in a mixing bowl then add eggs, fresh milk, vanilla extract, and olive oil to it. Whisk until incorporated.

4. Next, gradually pour the wet mixture into the dry mixture then fold it until combined.

5. Then, add blueberries to the batter. Mix until just combined.

6. Using an ice cream scoop or a soup ladle divide the batter into the prepared muffin tins then bake them for approximately 15 to 20 minutes or until it is light golden brown on top.

7. Next, check the doneness of the muffins by inserting a toothpick into the muffins then remove the muffins from the oven.

8. Let the muffins cool in the muffin tins for approximately 5 minutes then transfer them to a cooling rack.

9. Serve and enjoy.

**Melted Blueberry Lava Muffins**

This is a super easy yet tasty muffin. You can make a batch of it in the morning or make the double batches in your spare time and reheat them as a quick breakfast. Both are the same. As a variation, you can replace the blueberry preserves with other flavored preserves. Or you can substitute them with raisins, Choco chips, or other fillings that you like.

**Yield:** 10-12 muffins

**Cooking time:** 30 minutes

**Ingredients:**

- ¼ teaspoon salt
- 1 teaspoon baking powder
- ¼ cup granulated sugar
- 1½ cups multi-purpose flour
- 1 egg
- ½ cup fresh milk
- ¼ cup butter
- 1 teaspoon vanilla extract
- ½ cup blueberry preserves

**Instructions:**

1. Melt butter over low heat then let it cool.

2. Preheat an oven to 400°F (204°C) and prepare 12 muffin tins. Put a paper cup into each muffin tin and set aside.

3. Combine sugar with multi-purpose flour, baking powder, and salt then mix well.

4. In another bowl, whisk milk together with the melted butter, egg, and vanilla extract.

5. Next, gradually pour the wet mixture into the dry mixture then mix until combined.

6. Fill half of each muffin cup with the batter then add 2 teaspoons of blueberry preserves to every muffin cup.

7. Add the remaining batter to the muffin tins until ¾ full then bake the muffins for 20 to 25 minutes.

8. Once it is done, remove the muffins from the oven and let them rest for 5 minutes in the muffin tins.

9. Then, transfer the muffins to a cooling rack and let them cool.

10. Serve and enjoy.

**Blueberry Oatmeal Muffins**

What breakfast did you have this morning? Some people may answer it with oatmeal that is served with milk, maple syrup, and fruits on top. For sure, it is the most common way of people having oatmeal. How if there is another delicious way to enjoy the oatmeal? This muffin recipe is another way to eat oatmeal, maple syrup, milk, and fruits in a mealtime. The blueberry in this recipe is only a choice of fruit that you can have. If you want, you can replace it with strawberry, cranberry, or other fruits as your desired.

**Yield:** 10-12 muffins

**Cooking time:** 30 minutes

**Ingredients:**
- ½ cup fresh milk
- ½ cup maple syrup
- 1¼ cups multi-purpose flour
- ¼ teaspoon salt
- 1 teaspoon vanilla extract
- 1 teaspoon baking soda
- 2 eggs
- 2 tablespoons olive oil
- 1 tablespoon lemon juice
- 1 cup fresh blueberries
- 1 cup oats

**Instructions:**

1. First, preheat an oven to 350°F (177°C) and prepare 12 muffin tins. Put a paper cup into each muffin tin and set aside.

2. Place the multi-purpose flour, salt, and baking soda in a bowl then mix well.

3. In another bowl, add eggs together with maple syrup, vanilla extract, fresh milk, olive oil, and lemon juice then whisk until incorporated.

4. Next, gradually pour the wet mixture into the dry mixture then fold to combine.

5. Mix the fresh blueberries with the oats then stir in the mixture into the muffin batter.

6. Using a soup ladle divide the batter into the prepared muffin tins then bakes them in the preheated oven.

7. Once it is done, remove the muffins from the oven and let them rest in the muffin tins for 5 minutes.

8. Arrange the muffins on a cooling rack and serve.

9. Enjoy!

## Strawberry Milky Coconut Muffins

This muffin is so good. The coconut flour in this recipe absorbs the liquid very well, resulting in a fluffy texture of the muffin. In the meantime, the coconut milk used in the muffin gives a savory flavor that other muffins may not have. For the best result, it is suggested to use the full fat coconut milk because light coconut milk will not give a strong savory taste to the muffin. Fresh coconut milk is good. However, canned coconut milk is also welcome.

**Yield:** 10-12 muffins

**Cooking time:** 30 minutes

**Ingredients:**

- ¼ teaspoon salt
- 1½ teaspoons baking powder
- 1½ cups coconut flour
- ½ cup granulated sugar
- 2 eggs
- ¼ cup coconut milk
- ¼ cup coconut oil
- ¼ cup shredded coconut

**Filling:**
- 1 cup fresh strawberries

**Topping:**
- ¼ cup shredded coconut
- 3 tablespoons granulated sugar
- 1½ tablespoons salted butter
- ½ teaspoon cinnamon

**Instructions:**

1. Cut the strawberries into very small dices then set aside.

2. Preheat an oven to 350°F (177°C) and prepare 12 muffin tins. Put a paper cup into each muffin tin and set aside.

3. Combine coconut flour with baking powder and salt then mix well. Set aside.

4. In a separate bowl, place granulated sugar together with egg, coconut milk, and coconut oil. Stir until incorporated.

5. Next, gradually pour the wet mixture into the dry then mix until combined.

6. Add shredded coconut to the batter then using a spatula fold it until mixed.

7. Fill half of the muffin tins with batter then add a teaspoon of diced strawberries to it.

8. Cover the strawberries with batter until ¾ full then set aside.

9. Next, combine granulated sugar with cinnamon and shredded coconut then mix well.

10. Cut the salted butter into small cubes then add them to the topping mixture.

11. Using your fingers, mix the topping ingredients until

becoming crumbles then sprinkle them on the top of the muffins.

12. Insert the muffins into the preheated oven then bake them for approximately 18 to 20 minutes or until they are done. The top of the muffins will be light golden brown.

13. Remove the muffins from the oven and let them cool in the muffin tins for approximately 5 minutes. Transfer the muffins to a cooling rack.

14. Serve and enjoy.

## Cinnamon Nutmeg Firm Cranberry Muffins

This muffin is loaded with spices that make the muffin full of flavor. When you bake it, the whole house will smell delicious. Cranberry is used as an additional ingredient. If you don't want cranberry or if it is not available, you can replace it with another kind of berries, or you can simply remove it. The muffin will still taste delicious.

**Yield:** 10-12 muffins

**Cooking time:** 30 minutes

**Ingredients:**

- 1½ cups multi-purpose flour
- 1½ teaspoons baking powder

- A pinch of ground nutmeg
- A pinch of ground cinnamon
- A pinch of salt
- ¼ cup canola oil
- ¾ cup granulated sugar
- 2 eggs
- 1 teaspoon vanilla extract
- ½ cup fresh milk
- 1 cup chopped cranberries

**Instructions:**

1. First, preheat an oven to 400°F (204°C) and prepare 12 muffin tins. Put a paper cup into each muffin tin and set aside.

2. Mix the flour with baking powder, nutmeg, cinnamon, and salt then stir until combined.

3. In another bowl, combine the granulated sugar with eggs until smooth then pour canola oil, vanilla extract, and fresh milk into it. Mix until incorporated.

4. Next, gradually combine the wet mixture with the dry mixture then add chopped cranberries to the batter. Fold to combine.

5. Using an ice cream scoop fill the prepared muffin tins with the batter until ¾ full then insert the muffins into the preheated oven and bake them.

6. After 2- to 22 minutes, check the doneness of the muffins and once it is done, remove the muffins from the oven.

7. Then, let the muffins rest in the muffin tins for 5 minutes before taking them out then arrange them on a cooling rack.

8. Serve and enjoy.

## Fruity Date Strawberry Muffins

Using plant-based ingredients, this recipe is perfect for vegans. The dates and maple syrup used in this recipe perform as a natural and healthy sweetener. In the meantime, the flax seed and almond milk work to replace the function of eggs. There is no doubt that this muffin tastes delicious. If you are actually not a vegan, you can change the olive oil with butter. If you want to use eggs, you can remove the flax seed and almond milk, then put two eggs into the batter.

**Yield:** 10-12 muffins

**Cooking time:** 45 minutes

**Ingredients:**

- 1½ cups multi-purpose flour
- 1 teaspoon baking powder
- ¼ teaspoon salt
- ½ cup chopped strawberries
- 2 tablespoons pitted and chopped dates
- ¼ cup unsweetened orange juice
- 1 teaspoon vanilla extract

- ⅔ cup unsweetened almond milk
- 2 tablespoons ground flax
- 2 tablespoons maple syrup
- ¼ cup olive oil
- 3 tablespoons raisins

**Instructions:**

1. Place the chopped strawberries in a saucepan together with the chopped dates, unsweetened orange juice, and vanilla extract. Cook for approximately 3 minutes.

2. Remove the saucepan from the heat then gently mash the strawberry mixture. Let it cool and set aside.

3. In the meantime, combine the ground flax with the almond milk then stir until incorporated. Let it rest for a few minutes.

4. Next, preheat an oven to 350°F (177°C) and line 12 large muffin tins with paper cups. Set aside.

5. Combine the multi-purpose flour with salt and baking powder then mix well.

6. Whisk the mashed strawberry mixture with maple syrup and olive oil then stir until incorporated.

7. After that, pour the strawberry mixture over the dry mixture then mix the ingredients until combined.

8. Next, add raisins to the batter and fold to combine.

9. Divide the batter into the prepared muffin tins then bake them for 22 to 25 minutes or until the muffins are done.

10. Let the muffin rest in the muffin tins for 5 minutes then arrange them on a cooling rack.

11. Serve and enjoy.

## Orange Oatmeal Muffins

This orange muffin is soft, tender, and aromatic. It performs a delicious taste of sweet muffin, a health benefit of oatmeal, and a refreshing aroma of orange. If you want it to be more orange flavor, you can use orange-flavored yogurt. For the more tempting aroma, some people love to sprinkle ground cinnamon on top.

**Yield:** 10-12 muffins

**Cooking time:** 25 minutes

**Ingredients:**

- 1 cup multi-purpose flour
- 1 teaspoon baking powder
- ¼ teaspoon salt
- ½ teaspoon grated orange zest
- ¼ cup granulated sugar
- 1 egg
- ½ cup orange juice
- ½ cup plain yogurt
- 1 cup oatmeal

**Topping:**

- 3 tablespoons granulated sugar

**Instructions:**

1. First, preheat an oven to 425°F (218°C) and prepare 12 muffin tins. Put a paper cup into each muffin tin and set aside.

2. Add grated orange, salt, and baking soda to the multi-purpose flour then mix well. Set aside.

3. Place sugar in a mixing bowl then add the egg to the bowl. Whisk until smooth.

4. Pour orange juice and plain yogurt into the egg mixture then stir until incorporated.

5. Next, transfer the wet mixture to the dry mixture then stir well.

6. After that, add the oatmeal to the batter then using a spatula fold until combined.

7. Using a soup ladle or an ice cream scoop divide the batter into the prepared muffin tins then sprinkle granulated sugar on top.

8. Insert the muffins into the preheated oven and bake them for approximately 15 minutes or until the muffins are light golden brown and a stick inserted to the muffins comes out clean.

9. Remove the muffins from the oven and let them cool for 5 minutes in the muffin tins.

10. Serve and enjoy.

## Aromatic Cloves Apple Muffins

With real apples inside, this muffin does taste delicious. It offers you a soft muffin with a crunchy sensation of apple cubes. To make the apples stay fresh and crunchy without any color changing, it is suggested to drizzle some lemon juice over the apples right after cutting them into cubes. Another secret to this delicious muffin is by precisely measuring the ground clove. Ground clove truly gives a nice aroma. However, too much ground clove will only result in a too strong aroma that will ruin the taste of the muffin.

**Yield:** 10-12 muffins

**Cooking time:** 35 minutes

**Ingredients:**
- ¾ cup granulated sugar
- 1½ cups multi-purpose flour
- ¼ teaspoon ground cloves
- ½ teaspoon baking powder
- ½ teaspoon baking soda
- 2 eggs
- 1 teaspoon vanilla extract
- ½ cup margarine
- 2 apples

**Instructions:**

1. Melt the margarine over low heat then let it cool for a few minutes. Set aside.

2. Preheat an oven to 350°F (177°C) and line 12 muffin tins with paper cups. Set aside.

3. Add ground cloves, baking soda, and baking powder to the multi-purpose flour then stir until combined.

4. Whisk sugar with eggs until mixed then add melted margarine and vanilla extract to it. Stir until incorporated.

5. Next , gradually pour the wet mixture into the dry mixture then mix until combined. Set aside.

6. Peel and cut the apples into small cubes or thin slices then fold them into the batter. Mix well.

7. Divide the batter into the prepared muffin tins then bake them for approximately 15 minutes or until a toothpick inserted into the apple muffins comes out clean.

8. Then, remove the apple muffins from the oven and let them cool in the muffin tins for approximately 5 minutes.

9. Serve and enjoy.

## Cranberry Buttermilk Muffins

Famous with its ability to raise batter, buttermilk surely

helps this muffin to be fluffier and lighter than the other ones without buttermilk. As the result, this muffin will be soft, moist, and tender. In short, the buttermilk brings the muffin into perfection. If buttermilk is not available at the moment you want to bake the muffin; you can simply make it yourself by mixing fresh milk with lemon juice or vinegar. The result will be the same!

**Yield:** 10-12 muffins

**Cooking time:** 30 minutes

**Ingredients:**

- 1½ cups multi-purpose flour
- ½ cup granulated sugar
- ¾ cup buttermilk
- ½ teaspoon baking soda
- 1 teaspoon baking powder
- ¼ teaspoon salt
- 2 eggs
- ½ cup unsalted butter
- 1 cup fresh or frozen cranberries

**Topping:**

- 2 teaspoons powdered sugar

**Instructions:**

1. First, melt the unsalted butter over low heat then let it cool. Set aside.

2. Second, preheat an oven to 375°F and prepare 12 muffin tins. Line each muffin tin with a paper cup then set aside.

3. Add salt, baking soda, and baking powder to the multi-purpose flour then mix well.

4. In another mixing bowl, place granulated sugar together with eggs then whisk until incorporated.

5. Add buttermilk and melted butter to the sugar and egg mixture then stir until incorporated.

6. Next, after that, pour the wet mixture into the dry mixture then mix well.

7. Stir in the cranberries to the batter then fold them until just combined.

8. Spoon the batter to the prepared muffin tins then bake them for 20 to 25 minutes or until they are done.

9. Insert a toothpick deeply into the muffins to check the doneness of the muffins then remove the muffins from the oven.

10. Let the muffins cool in the muffins tins then transfer them to a cooling rack.

11. Dust the powdered sugar over the muffins and serve.

12. Enjoy!

## Lemon Butter Muffins with Choco Chips

This lemon muffin may sound simple. However, it truly tastes delicious. The grated lemon zest adds flavor to this muffin so that you can easily get a tasty citrusy muffin. To avoid a distraction to the lemon aroma, it is best not to add any other flavor to the muffin, such as vanilla, lychee, cinnamon, etc. However, additional Chocolate chips, dried raisins, or grated coconut are acceptable since they are improving the appearance and texture of the muffin.

**Yield:** 10-12 muffins

**Cooking time:** 25 minutes

**Ingredients:**

- 1½ cups multi-purpose flour
- 1 teaspoon baking powder
- ½ teaspoon grated lemon zest
- ¾ cup caster sugar
- ½ cup plain yogurt
- 3 tablespoons lemon juice
- 1½ tablespoons butter
- ¼ cup less sweet Choco chips

**Instructions:**

1. First, melt the butter over low heat. Then, let it cool.

2. Preheat an oven to 350°F (177°C) and prepare 12 muffin tins. Put a paper cup into each muffin tin and set aside.

3. Combine the multi-purpose flour with baking powder and grated lemon zest then add caster sugar to the mixture. Mix well.

4. Add lemon juice and melted butter to the plain yogurt then stir until incorporated.

5. Pour the wet mixture over the dry mixture then whisk until combined.

6. Stir in Choco chips to the batter then mix well.

7. Next, using an ice cream scoop spoon the batter and fill the prepared muffin tins ¾ full.

8. Insert the muffins to the preheated oven and bake them for 20 minutes or until a toothpick inserted into the muffins comes out clean.

9. Once it is done, remove the muffins from the oven and let them rest in the muffin tins for 5 minutes.

10. Transfer the muffins to a cooling rack. Then, let them cool.

11. Serve and enjoy.

**Coconut Lemon Muffins with Poppy Seeds**

Coconut flour is considered as healthy flour that is solely made from coconut. The flour is rich in fiber, which promotes good digestion. Besides, it also helps to boost weight loss, maintain stable blood sugar, and improve heart health. For sure, coconut flour is a good option for those who care about health. Unfortunately, sometimes, coconut flour is not easy to find. If it happens, you can make homemade coconut flour by baking coconut pulp until it is dried, then process it in a food processor into a fine powder.

**Yield:** 10-12 muffins

**Cooking time:** 25 minutes

**Ingredients:**

- 1¼ cups coconut flour
- 1 teaspoon baking powder
- ¼ teaspoon salt
- 1 teaspoon grated lemon zest
- ¼ cup granulated sugar
- 1 egg
- 2 tablespoons margarine
- 2 tablespoons vegetable oil
- ½ cup coconut milk
- 2 tablespoons lemon juice
- 1 teaspoon lemon extract
- ¼ cup unsweetened shredded coconut
- 1 tablespoon poppy seeds

**Instructions:**

1. First, melt the margarine then let it cool.

2. Second, preheat an oven to 450°F (232°C) and prepare 12 muffin tins. Put a paper cup into each muffin tin and set aside.

3. Combine the coconut flour with baking powder, salt, and grated lemon zest then set aside.

4. In another bowl, whisk the granulated sugar with the egg until smooth and creamy then pour melted margarine, vegetable oil, coconut oil, lemon juice, and lemon extract into it. Stir until incorporated.

5. Next, gradually pour the wet mixture into the dry mixture then mix well.

6. Add unsweetened shredded coconut together with poppy seeds to the batter then fold until combined.

7. Using an ice cream scoop divide the batter into the prepared muffin tins then insert them into the preheated

oven and bake the muffins.

8. Next, after 5 minutes, reduce the temperature of the oven to 350°F (177°C) then continues baking the muffins for 14 to 17 minutes.

9. Once it is done, remove the muffins from the oven and let them rest in the muffin tins for 5 minutes.

10. Take the muffins out of the tins then transfer them to a cooling rack.

11. Serve and enjoy.

## Apricot Butter Moist Muffins

Once you have baked this muffin, you will definitely make it again. This apricot muffin is a fun variation of muffin, which offers a refreshing and tempting apricot flavor. The muffin itself has already tasted good. However, to enhance its taste and appearance, you can sprinkle chopped almonds or many other kinds of nuts on top.

**Yield:** 10-12 muffins

**Cooking time:** 25 minutes

**Ingredients:**

- ¼ cup butter
- ½ cup powdered sugar

- 1 egg
- ¼ teaspoon salt
- 1 teaspoon apricot essence
- ¼ cup whipping cream
- 1¼ cups multi-purpose flour
- 1 teaspoon baking powder
- 1 teaspoon ground cinnamon
- ½ cup chopped dried apricots

**Instructions:**

1. Preheat an oven to 325°F (191°C) and prepare 12 muffin tins. Put a paper cup into each muffin tin and set aside.

2. Place the butter in a mixing bowl then using an electric mixer softens the butter.

3. Add sugar to the softened butter then beat until smooth and creamy.

4. Crack the egg then drop it together with apricot essence and whipped cream into the mixing bowl. Beat until incorporated then remove the mixer.

5. In another bowl, combine the multi-purpose flour with cinnamon, salt, and baking powder then mix well.

6. Add the multi-purpose flour to the wet mixture then using a spatula mix until combined.

7. Stir in the chopped dried apricots to the batter then fold to combine.

8. Using an ice cream scoop divide the batter into the prepared muffin tins then bakes them.

9. Once the muffins are done, remove them from the oven and let the muffins rest in the muffin tins for 5 minutes.

10. Transfer the muffins to a cooling rack. Then, let them cool.

11. Serve and enjoy.

## Pineapple Muffins with Cookie Topping

This muffin is unique. It performs a soft texture inside but crispy crunch on top. It is more like a collaboration between a muffin and a cookie. First, you need to make the muffin, then cover it with the cookie dough and bake the muffin again until the top of the muffin is light golden brown. If it is available, sprinkle chopped nuts or other topping options will surely give a better look to the muffin.

**Yield:** 10-12 muffins

**Cooking time:** 25 minutes

**Ingredients:**

- 1 cup multi-purpose flour
- ¼ teaspoon baking soda
- ½ teaspoon baking powder
- A pinch of salt
- ¼ teaspoon grated lemon zest
- ½ cup granulated sugar
- 1 egg
- ¼ cup vegetable oil
- ½ cup plain yogurt

- ½ cup diced canned pineapples

**Topping:**
- ¼ cup butter
- ½ cup multi-purpose flour
- 2 tablespoons powdered sugar
- 1 egg
- A pinch of cloves

**Instructions:**

1. First, preheat an oven to 350°F (177°C) and prepare 12 muffin tins. Put a paper cup into each muffin tin and set aside.

2. Combine the multi-purpose flour with baking soda, baking powder, salt, and grated lemon zest then mix well.

3. Whisk the granulated sugar with eggs then add plain yogurt and vegetable oil to the mixture. Mix well.

4. Next, transfer the wet mixture to the dry mixture then using a spatula mix it until incorporated.

5. Stir in the diced pineapples to the batter then fold until combined.

6. Using an ice cream scoop, carefully divide the batter into the prepared muffin tins then bake the muffins for 20-25 minutes or until a toothpick inserted deeply into the muffins comes out clean.

7. Next, remove the muffins from the oven and let them cool. Do not take the muffins out of the muffin tins.

8. In the meantime, soften the butter then mix it with sugar, egg, and flour.

9. Knead the topping ingredients until becoming dough then using a rolling pin rolls the dough into a ¼-inch thickness layer.

10. Using a circle mold cut the thin dough then places each round-dough on each muffin.

11. Preheat the oven on upper heat to 325°F (163°C) then returns the muffins with topping to the oven.

12. Bake the muffins for approximately 10 minutes or until the topping is lightly golden brown and cracked.

13. Then, remove the muffins from the oven and let them rest in the muffin tins for 5 minutes.

14. Transfer the muffins to a cooling rack and serve.

15. Enjoy!

## Soymilk Real Apple Muffins

Probably, you have never tried soymilk for making muffins. Here comes a muffin recipe that is easy and trusty. Surprise! Once you try this, you will get an amazing muffin with a spongy and moist texture. The ground cinnamon is this recipe also helps to make this muffin more tempting and aromatic. If you like a little warm sensation, you can add a pinch of ground ginger to the muffin.

**Yield:** 10-12 muffins

**Cooking time:** 35 minutes

**Ingredients:**

- 1½ cups self-raising flour
- 1 teaspoon ground cinnamon
- ½ cup brown sugar
- 3 tablespoons granulated sugar
- 1 egg
- ¾ cup unsweetened soymilk
- ½ cup vegetable oil
- 2 apples
- 2 tablespoons lemon juice

**Instructions:**

1. Core the apples. Then, cut them into thin slices wedges.

2. Rub the sliced apples with lemon juice then set aside.

3. Preheat an oven to 360°F (182°C) and prepare 12 muffin tins. Put a paper cup into each muffin tin and set aside.

4. Place the brown sugar in a mixing bowl together with granulated sugar and ground cinnamon then mix well.

5. Add egg to the sugar mixture then pour unsweetened soymilk and vegetable oil to it. Whisk until smooth.

6. Stir in the self-raising flour to the mixture then mix well.

7. Add the sliced apples to the batter then fold until combined.

8. Using an ice cream scoop divide the batter into the prepared muffin tins then insert the muffins into the oven and bake them.

9. After 20 minutes, check the doneness of the muffins and insert a toothpick into the muffins. If the toothpick comes out clean, it means that the muffins are done.

10. Remove the muffins from the oven and let them rest in the tins for 5 minutes.

11. Take the muffins out of the tins and transfer them to a cooling rack.

12. Serve and enjoy.

## Orange Chocolate Muffins

The chocolate and orange combination is true magic. They have a contrasting taste in which the chocolate is rich and fatty, while the orange is fruity and fresh. Surprisingly, this collaboration brings the amazing result! This muffin tastes so good! Another fun fact is that according to the directions, this beautiful muffin is easy to make. You can make the whole batter first and give flavor later. To make the same amount of batter between the two flavors, it is suggested to measure the batter, so you can have exactly half of the batter with one color. However, if that kind of thing does not bother you, you can divide the batter according to your desire.

**Yield:** 10-12 muffins

**Cooking time:** 35 minutes

**Ingredients:**

- ⅓ cup butter
- 2 eggs
- ¾ cup granulated sugar

- ¼ cup sour cream
- ¼ cup orange yogurt
- 1 tablespoon grated orange zest
- 1½ cups multi-purpose flour
- ¼ teaspoon salt
- 2 tablespoons unsweetened cocoa powder
- ¼ cup Choco chips

**Instructions:**

1. Melt the butter over low heat. Then, let it cool.

2. Preheat an oven to 360°F (182°C) and prepare 12 muffin tins. Put a paper cup into each muffin tin and set aside.

3. Combine the multi-purpose flour with baking powder, grated orange zest, and salt then mix well.

4. In another bowl, whisk the granulated sugar with eggs then stir in sour cream, orange yogurt, and melted butter to the bowl. Mix until incorporated.

5. Mix the wet mixture with the dry mixture then fold to combine.

6. Take about a half of the batter then add cocoa powder to it. Mix well.

7. Fill each prepared muffin tin with both orange and chocolate batter then insert the muffins into the preheated oven.

8. Sprinkle Choco chips on top and bake the muffins for approximately 15 to 20 minutes or until a toothpick inserted deeply into the muffins comes out clean.

9. Once it is done, remove the muffins from the oven and let them rest in the tins for 5 minutes.

10. Take the muffins out of the tins and let them cool on a cooling rack.

11. Serve and enjoy.

## Almond Muffins with Poppy Seeds

Once you try this recipe, you will confess that this muffin is completely fluffy. It is the almond flour that works as a raising agent, while the almond essence plays a role as the source of tempting flavor. For this super light muffin, it is perfect for a little morning treat. Don't forget about the poppy seed. It offers a package of healthy nutrients, such as fiber, calcium, iron, zinc, protein, and good fats. Not to mention, the antioxidant in the poppy seed will reduce the risk of having cancer.

**Yield:** 10-12 muffins

**Cooking time:** 25 minutes

**Ingredients:**

- ¼ teaspoon salt
- 1 teaspoon baking powder
- ¾ cup almond flour
- ¾ cup multi-purpose flour
- ¾ cup sour cream
- ½ cup granulated sugar
- 1 egg

- 2 tablespoons unsweetened almond milk
- 1 teaspoon almond extract
- ¼ cup butter
- 2 tablespoons poppy seeds

**Instructions:**

1. Melt the butter over medium heat. Then, let it cool. Set aside.

2. Next, preheat an oven to 350°F (177°C) and prepare 12 muffin tins. Put a paper cup into each muffin tin and set aside.

3. Mix the multi-purpose flour with almond flour, baking powder, and salt then stir until combined.

4. In another bowl, whisk the granulated sugar with egg then pour sour cream, almond milk, almond extract, and melted butter to it. Mix well.

5. Next, gradually combine the wet mixture with the dry mixture then add poppy seeds to the batter. Fold until combined.

6. Using a soup ladle divide the batter into the prepared muffin tins then insert them into the preheated oven and bake the muffins.

7. Once the muffins are done, carefully remove them from the oven and let them cool on a cooling rack.

8. Serve and enjoy.

## Cappuccino Almond Walnuts Muffins

Just like a cup of cappuccino, this muffin offers you a creamy muffin with coffee flavor. Because this muffin uses almond flour and almond milk as the main ingredients, it doesn't taste heavy at all. Therefore, it is not only best for breakfast or any other main meals but also dessert or snack. For the best snacking time, the muffin is perfect to be enjoyed with a cup of iced coffee milk.

**Yield:** 10-12 muffins

**Cooking time:** 30 minutes

**Ingredients:**

- 1½ cups almond flour
- 1½ teaspoons baking powder
- ¼ teaspoon salt
- ¾ cup walnut crumbles
- ¾ cup brown sugar
- 1 egg
- ¾ cup unsweetened almond milk
- ¼ cup espresso
- ½ cup butter

**Instructions:**

1. Melt butter over low heat then let it cool.

2. Preheat an oven to 400°F (204°C) and line 12 muffin tins with paper cups. Set aside.

3. Combine the almond flour with salt and baking powder then mix well.

4. Add ½ cup of walnut crumbles then mix it with the flour mixture. Set aside.

5. Whisk brown sugar with the egg until dissolved then adds milk, espresso, and melted butter to it. Stir until incorporated.

6. Pour the wet mixture into the dry mixture then stir until combined.

7. Next, using a soup ladle or an ice cream scoop, divide the batter into the prepared muffin tins then sprinkle the remaining walnut crumbles on top.

8. Insert the muffin tins into the preheated oven and bake the muffins for 15 to 20 minutes. Prick a toothpick into the muffins and check the doneness of the muffins.

9. Once the muffins are done, carefully remove them from the oven. Then, let them cool for 5 minutes in the muffin tins.

10. Take them out of the muffin tins. Then, arrange them on a cooling rack.

11. Serve and enjoy.

## Pecan Moist Muffins with Honey Glaze

Pecan muffin or moist muffin is probably easy to find. However, the one with tempting honey glaze is special. Make sure not to over-bake the muffin after it is being glazed. The over-baked muffin will taste bitter because the glaze mixture is easy to be burnt. But the perfect one tastes delicious. As a variation, you can drizzle vanilla icing on top.

**Yield:** 10-12 muffins

**Cooking time:** 30 minutes

**Ingredients:**
- ¼ cup butter
- 6 tablespoons brown sugar
- 3 tablespoons honey
- 2 tablespoons eggs
- 1 teaspoon vanilla
- ½ cup multi-purpose flour
- ½ teaspoon baking powder
- ¼ teaspoon salt
- ¾ cup pecan crumbles

**Glaze:**
- 2 tablespoons butter
- 2 tablespoons honey

- ¼ cup brown sugar

**Instructions:**

1. First, preheat an oven to 425°F (218°C) and line 12 muffin tins with paper cups. Set aside.

2. Place butter and brown sugar in a mixing bowl then using an electric mixer beat until smooth and creamy.

3. Add honey, eggs, and vanilla to the creamy mixture then beat until fluffy.

4. Combine the multi-purpose flour with baking powder and salt then add the mixture to the butter mixture. Slowly beat the batter.

5. Next, stir in the pecan crumbles to the batter then using a spatula fold until combined.

6. Divide the batter into the prepared muffin tins then bake them.

7. Then, in the meantime, combine the topping ingredients in a bowl then mix well.

8. Once the muffins are done, baste the glaze mixture on top of the muffins then bake again for 3 minutes or until the glaze is just melted.

9. Remove the muffins from the oven and let them rest for 5 minutes in the muffin tins.

10. Continue letting the muffins cool on a cooling rack and serve.

11. Enjoy!

### Buttermilk Peanut Palm Sugar Muffins

Palm sugar is a sweetener that contains many good minerals but zero fats and protein. Because of the natural making process, the nutrition in palm sugar remains maintained, causing it becomes a healthy choice of sugar. Also, by using palm sugar, you will not need to add any food coloring. It brings natural brown color to muffins. For sure, palm sugar is a perfect choice of sweetener.

**Yield:** 10-12 muffins

**Cooking time:** 40 minutes

**Ingredients:**

- 1 cup roasted peanuts
- ½ cup palm sugar
- 2 eggs
- ¾ cup buttermilk
- ¼ cup vegetable oil
- 1½ cups multi-purpose flour
- ½ teaspoon baking soda
- 1 teaspoon baking powder
- 1 teaspoon vanilla extract

**Instructions:**

1. First, place the roasted peanuts in a food processor then process until becoming crumbles. Set aside.

2. Preheat an oven to 400°F (204°C) and prepare 12 muffin tins. Put a paper cup into each muffin tin then set aside.

3. Whisk the eggs together with the palm sugar until fluffy then add buttermilk, vegetable oil, and vanilla extract. Stir well.

4. In another bowl, combine the multi-purpose flour with baking powder and baking soda then mix well. Sift the flour.

5. Next, pour the wet mixture into the dry mixture then mix until incorporated.

6. Stir in the peanut crumbles to the batter then fold to combine.

7. Divide the batter into the prepared muffin tins then insert them into the preheated oven. Bake the muffins.

8. Once it is done, remove the muffins from the oven and let them rest in the muffin tins for 5 minutes.

9. Transfer the muffins to a cooling rack and let them cool.

10. Serve and enjoy.

## Mixed Nutty Muffins with Cinnamon

This muffin is dedicated to nut lovers. It tastes very nutty with crunchy hazelnut on top. Besides, this muffin also uses macadamia oil that surely enhances the nutty flavor. For this very flexible recipe, you can replace the peanuts with another kind of nuts, as you desire. However, it is not suggested to substitute the macadamia oil with other oil. For sure, macadamia oil has lots of health benefits that are too good to skip.

**Yield:** 10-12 muffins

**Cooking time:** 40 minutes

**Ingredients:**

- ½ teaspoon baking powder
- ½ teaspoon baking soda
- ¾ teaspoon ground cinnamon
- 1½ cups multi-purpose flour
- 1 egg
- ¼ cup sugar
- ¾ cup unsweetened almond milk
- 1 teaspoon vanilla extract
- ¼ cup macadamia oil
- ½ cup peanut crumbles

**Topping:**

- ¼ cup chopped hazelnuts

**Instructions:**

1. First, preheat an oven to 350°F (177°C) and prepare 12 muffin tins. Put a paper cup into each muffin tin then set aside.

2. Combine multi-purpose flour with baking soda, baking powder, and cinnamon then mix well.

3. In another bowl, whisk the egg with sugar then pour

almond milk, vanilla extract, and macadamia oil into the mixture. Stir until incorporated.

4. Next, gradually mix the wet mixture with the dry mixture then add peanut crumbles to the batter. Fold to combine.

5. Using a soup ladle or an ice cream scoop divide the batter into the prepared muffin tins then sprinkle chopped hazelnuts on top.

6. Bake the muffins in the preheated oven and once a toothpick inserted to the muffins comes out clean, remove them from the oven.

7. Then, let the muffins rest in the muffin tins for 5 minutes before taking them out of the muffin tins. Transfer them to a cooling rack.

8. Serve and enjoy.

## Cocoa Black Beans Muffins with Maple Syrup

What is your consideration when you are making a muffin? This question may not be easy to answer, especially when kids will be the main customer of this muffin. For sure, health content will become your focus. This muffin is an easy-to-make muffin with a bunch of protein and fiber. It is a kind of snack, breakfast, lunch, or dinner that your kids will surely like it. Made with black beans, which have been known as a nutritious legume, this muffin is absolutely good for your kids. Don't forget about the natural chocolate flavor from the cocoa and the creamy but light texture from the almond milk. Surely, your kids will love the muffin.

**Yield:** 10-12 muffins

**Cooking time:** 40 minutes

**Ingredients:**

- 1 cup canned and rinsed black beans
- 2 eggs
- ½ cup unsweetened cocoa powder
- ¾ teaspoon baking powder
- ½ cup brown sugar
- ¼ cup maple syrup
- 2 tablespoons unsweetened almond milk
- 2 tablespoons olive oil

**Instructions:**

1. First, preheat an oven to 350°F (177°C) and prepare 12 muffin tins. Put a paper cup into each muffin tin then set aside.

2. Place the entire ingredients--black beans, eggs, cocoa powder, baking powder, brown sugar, maple syrup, almond milk, and olive oil in a blender then blend until smooth and incorporated.

3. Next, using a soup ladle divide the batter into the prepared muffin tins then insert them in the preheated oven and bake the muffins.

4. After 15 minutes, check the muffins and insert a tooth-pick into the muffins.

5. Once the toothpick comes out clean, remove the muffins from the oven and let them rest in the muffin tins for 5 minutes.

6. Take the muffins out the tins then arrange them on a cooling rack.

7. Serve and enjoy.

**Cheesy Parsley Muffins with Garlic Aroma**

This cheesy muffin is great to eat in the morning or as a yummy snack during the day. Served with cheese cubes inside and grated cheese on top, this muffin offers an ultimate cheesy taste in every single bite. If you want another sensation of cheese, you can remove the grated cheddar cheese on top and replace it with grated mozzarella cheese. The mozzarella cheese will be melted and make your tongue dance. Don't forget about the role of the parsley. It mingles well with the cheese resulting in an appetizing aroma. That is why; it is not recommended to skip the parsley.

**Yield:** 10-12 muffins

**Cooking time:** 35 minutes

**Ingredients:**

- 1½ cups self-raising flour
- 2 teaspoons dried parsley
- ½ cup cheddar cheese cubes
- 2 tablespoons grated Parmesan cheese
- 1 egg
- 1 teaspoon minced garlic
- ¾ cup fresh milk
- 3 tablespoons plain yogurt
- 3 tablespoons vegetable oil
- 2 tablespoons margarine

**Topping:**
- Grated Cheddar Cheese
- Diced fresh parsley

**Instructions:**

1. Melt the margarine over low heat then let it cool.

2. Preheat an oven to 350°F (177°C) and prepare 12 muffin tins. Put a paper cup into each muffin tin then set aside.

3. Whisk the egg with Parmesan cheese, minced garlic, fresh milk, plain yogurt, vegetable oil, and melted margarine then add self-raising flour to the mixture. Mix well.

4. Add the cheddar cheese cubes and dried parsley to the batter then fold until combined.

5. Using an ice cream scoop divide the batter into the prepared muffin tins then sprinkle grated cheddar cheese and parsley on top.

6. Insert the muffins into the preheated oven then bake the muffins for 20-30 minutes.

7. Once the muffins are done and a toothpick inserted deeply into the muffins comes out clean, carefully remove the muffins from the oven.

8. Let the muffins rest in the tins for 5 minutes then take them out and transfer them to a cooling rack.

9. Serve and enjoy.

## Buttermilk Cheddar Muffins with Sunflower Oil

Made from organic sunflower seed that is pressed well, sunflower oil is truly a good option of oil to be involved in a baking muffin. The sunflower oil boosts the good fat content that makes your heart healthier. Besides, it is also rich in vitamin E and antioxidants that surely keep your immune system better and stronger. More than that, sunflower oil is gluten-free. In its collaboration with cheese, these two make a perfect taste and texture of these muffins.

**Yield:** 10-12 muffins

**Cooking time:** 30 minutes

**Ingredients:**

- 2 cups self-raising flour
- 1½ teaspoons paprika
- 2 teaspoons Italian seasoning
- 1 cup grated cheddar cheese
- 2 eggs
- ¼ cup powdered sugar

- ½ cup buttermilk
- ½ cup sunflower oil

**Instructions:**

1. First, preheat an oven to 350°F (177°C) and prepare 12 muffin tins. Put a paper cup into each muffin tin then set aside.

2. Mix the self-raising flour with paprika and Italian seasoning then set aside.

3. Whisk the eggs with powdered sugar until smooth then pour buttermilk and sunflower oil into it.

4. Next, gradually add the dry mixture to the wet mixture then mix until incorporated.

5. After that, stir in the grated cheddar cheese then fold to combine.

6. Using an ice cream scoop divide the batter into the prepared muffin tins then insert them into the preheated oven and bake the muffins.

7. Check the doneness of the muffins after 20 minutes of baking and insert a toothpick into them.

8. Once the toothpick comes out clean, remove the muffins from the oven and let them rest in the tins for 5 minutes.

9. Take the muffins out of the tins and arrange them on a cooling rack.

10. Serve and enjoy.

## Almond Milk Cream Cheese Muffins

There is no doubt that almond and cheese never fail. The combination of those two is really good. Even it can be said as too good. This muffin offers a soft and fluffy muffin with a semi-sweet cheesy taste. Surely, everyone will love it! For the best result, it is not suggested to replace any kind of ingredients of the recipe. However, there is still a chance to vary the muffin. If you like, you can add raisins, Choco chips, sliced almonds, and many other additional toppings or fillings. As long as it will not affect the batter, the muffin will be fine.

**Yield:** 10-12 muffins

**Cooking time:** 30 minutes

**Ingredients:**

- 2 cups almond flour
- 1 teaspoon baking powder
- ¼ teaspoon salt
- ¾ cup granulated sugar
- ½ cup softened cream cheese
- 1 egg
- ⅓ cup unsweetened almond milk
- ¼ cup vegetable oil
- ½ cup grated cheddar cheese

**Instructions:**

1. Preheat an oven to 325°F (191°C) and prepare 12 muffin tins. Put a paper cup into each muffin tin then set aside.

2. Combine the almond flour with salt and baking powder then sift the flour mixture and set aside.

3. Place sugar, softened cream cheese, and egg in a mixing bowl then using an electric mixer beat until fluffy.

4. Alternately add the flour mixture, almond milk, and vegetable oil to the mixture then beat to combine.

5. Using a soup ladle fill each prepared muffin tin with the batter until ¾ full then sprinkle grated cheddar cheese on top.

6. Insert the muffins into the preheated oven and bake them for 24-30 minutes.

7. Once it is done, remove the muffins from the oven and let them rest in the tins for 5 minutes. The muffins will be firm and light golden brown.

8. Take the muffins out of the tins then arrange them on a cooling rack.

9. Serve and enjoy.

## Cheesy Muffins with Chocolate Jam Marble

This marble muffin is very easy to make but so impressive to serve. The key to the beautiful pattern is to not over blend the batter. If you blend the batter too much, you will end up with a light brown color of muffin. To enhance both the taste and the appearance of the muffin, you can add cream cheese frosting on top. It will not only make the muffin more tempting but also prettier. More than that, it may also increase the price!

**Yield:** 10-12 muffins

**Cooking time:** 30 minutes

**Ingredients:**
- 1½ cups multi-purpose flour
- 3 tablespoons sugar
- ¾ teaspoon baking powder
- ¼ teaspoon salt
- 1½ cups grated cheddar cheese
- ¾ cup plain yogurt
- 3 tablespoons olive oil
- 1 egg
- ½ cup chocolate jam

**Instructions:**
1. First, preheat an oven to 350°F (177°C) and prepare 12 muffin tins. Put a paper cup into each muffin tin then set aside.

2. Stir the multi-purpose flour with sugar, baking powder, and salt then set aside.

3. In another bowl, crack the egg then mix it with yogurt and olive oil.

4. Next, gradually combine the wet mixture with the dry mixture then mix well.

5. Using an ice cream scoop divide the batter into the prepared muffin tins until ¾ full and drop a tablespoon of chocolate jam into each muffin.

6. Using a thin stick swirl each muffin to make a marble texture then insert the muffins into the preheated oven.

7. Next, bake the muffins for approximately 20 to 25 minutes and check the doneness by inserting a toothpick into the muffins.

8. Once it is done or the toothpick comes out clean, remove the muffins from the oven and let them rest in the muffin tins for 5 minutes.

9. Take the muffins out of the tins then transfer them to a cooling rack.

10. Serve and enjoy.

## Brown Sugar Pumpkin Muffins

You may not actually be a big fan of pumpkin. However, once you try this muffin, you will definitely change the way you look at a pumpkin. This recipe is super-flavorful with brown sugar and pumpkin pie spice as the hero. The brown sugar in the recipe may be limited because too much sugar will only cause a too-much sweet muffin that surely not everyone's favorite. However, you can always play with the pumpkin pie spice. It may be added or adjusted according to your desire. To enhance the aroma, some people like to add ground cinnamon to the batter, while coarse sugar on top will be an alternative to make the muffin more appetizing.

**Yield:** 10-12 muffins

**Cooking time:** 30 minutes

**Ingredients:**

- 1 cup multi-purpose flour
- 2 teaspoons pumpkin pie spice
- ¼ teaspoon salt
- 1 teaspoon baking soda
- ¼ cup granulated sugar
- 2 tablespoons brown sugar
- 2 eggs
- ¾ cup canned pumpkin puree
- 3 tablespoons coconut oil
- 3 tablespoons lemon juice
- ½ teaspoon grated lemon zest

**Instructions:**

1. First, preheat an oven to 350°F (177°C) and prepare 12 muffin tins.

2. Place a paper cup in each muffin tin then set aside.

3. Mix the multi-purpose flour with pumpkin pie spice, baking soda, and salt then stir until combined. Set aside.

4. In a separate mixing bowl combine granulated sugar with brown sugar, eggs, canned pumpkin puree, coconut oil, lemon juice, and grated lemon zest then stir until incorporated.

5. Next, gradually pour the wet mixture into the dry mixture then whisk until well combined.

6. Divide the batter into the prepared muffin tins then bake the muffins for 20 minutes or until the muffins are done. Insert a toothpick into a muffin to check if the muffin is done.

7. Remove the pumpkin muffins from the oven and let them cool in the muffin tins for 5 minutes.

8. Take the pumpkin muffins out of the tins then arrange them on a cooling rack.

9. Serve and enjoy.

## Brown Sugar Muffins with Cinnamon Aroma

This is an awesome muffin that is very easy to make. It uses common ingredients that are usually available in your kitchen. Don't worry; although this muffin sounds to be just like that, the taste is awesome. If you like a little crunch with the muffin, you can add some chopped nuts to the muffin. However, it is recommended only to add not more than ¼ cup of chopped nuts to the batter. It is the perfect amount of nuts that will not ruin the batter. The measurement works the same way with dried fruits or chocolate chips.

**Yield:** 10-12 muffins

**Cooking time:** 30 minutes

**Ingredients:**

- 1 cup multi-purpose flour
- ¼ teaspoon ground cloves
- ¼ teaspoon salt
- ¾ teaspoon ground cinnamon
- 1 teaspoon baking powder
- ⅔ cup fresh milk
- ⅔ cup brown sugar
- 2 tablespoons vegetable oil
- 2 eggs

**Instructions:**

1. First, preheat an oven to 425°F (218°C) and prepare 12 muffin tins. Put a paper cup into each muffin tin then set aside.

2. Add cinnamon, cloves, salt, and baking powder to the flour then mix well.

3. In another bowl, combine brown sugar with egg and milk then stir until incorporated.

4. Add vegetable oil to the wet mixture then mix until combined.

5. Next, pour the wet mixture into the dry mixture then fold it until combined.

6. Divide the mixture into the prepared muffin tins then bake them for 20 to 25 minutes or until a toothpick inserted to the muffins comes out clean.

7. Remove the muffins from the oven. Then, allow them

to cool in the muffin tins for approximately 5 minutes then transfer the muffins to a cooling rack.

8. Serve and enjoy.

**Spiced Pumpkin Muffins with Molasses**

It has to admit that spices play a big role in this muffin. Without all the spices, this muffin wouldn't be complete. That is why; it highly recommended not skipping any spices from the muffin. The pumpkin does offer health benefits and moist texture. However, it is the spice that gives flavor. If you want some variations into this muffin, you can add nuts, chocolate chips, dried fruits, or other seeds.

**Yield:** 10-12 muffins

**Cooking time:** 30 minutes

**Ingredients:**

- 1 teaspoon ground cinnamon
- 1 teaspoon baking soda
- 1½ cups multi-purpose flour
- ¼ teaspoon salt
- ¼ teaspoon ground ginger
- A pinch of ground nutmeg
- A pinch of allspice

- ¼ cup brown sugar
- 2 tablespoons molasses
- 1 egg
- ¼ cup buttermilk
- 1 teaspoon vanilla extract
- ½ cup canned pumpkin puree
- 3 tablespoons olive oil
- ¼ cup pumpkin seeds

**Instructions:**

1. First, preheat an oven to 400°F (204°C) and prepare 12 muffin tins. Put a paper cup into each muffin tin then set aside.

2. Season the multi-purpose flour with salt; cinnamon, ginger, and allspice then mix well.

3. Add baking soda to the multi-purpose flour mixture then mix well. Sift the flour.

4. In another bowl, place the brown sugar together with molasses then add egg and vanilla extract to it. Whisk until incorporated.

5. Next, pour olive oil and pumpkin puree into the sugar mixture then mix well.

6. After that, mix the wet mixture with the dry mixture then fold until combined.

7. Using an ice cream scoop fill each prepared muffin tins until ¾ full then sprinkle pumpkin seeds on top.

8. Insert the muffins into the preheated oven then bake them for 18 to 20 minutes.

9. Once it is done, remove the muffins from the oven and let them rest for 5 minutes in the muffin tins.

10. Transfer the muffins to a cooling rack. Then, let them

cool.

11. Serve and enjoy.

## Broccoli Muffins with Maple Syrup Sweetener

There is no purpose to manipulate, but this muffin is the best way to sneak broccoli. The muffin tastes so delicious, which no one will notice that there is some extra vegetable inside. For sure, this muffin is good for everyone, including the kids. Any kind of vegetables can be used here. You can substitute the broccoli with carrot, Bok Choi, spinach, etc. Or, you may also mix some of the veggies. If you want to have a chocolate veggie muffin, you can replace half of the multi-purpose flour with cocoa powder.

**Yield:** 10-12 muffins

**Cooking time:** 35 minutes

**Ingredients:**

- 1 cup chopped broccoli
- ¾ cup unsweetened almond milk
- 1½ tablespoons apple cider vinegar
- 1½ teaspoons vanilla extract
- ⅓ cup maple syrup
- ⅓ cup vegetable oil

- ½ cup multi-purpose flour
- 1½ cups quick-cooking oats
- 1 teaspoon baking powder
- ½ teaspoon baking soda
- ¼ teaspoon salt
- 1 teaspoon ground cinnamon
- 3 tablespoons diced chocolate compound

**Instructions:**

1. Preheat an oven 350°F (177°C) and prepare 12 muffin tins. Put a paper cup into each muffin tin then set aside.

2. Place the chopped broccoli in a blender then add almond milk, apple cider vinegar, vanilla extract, vegetable oil, and maple syrup. Process the ingredients until smooth.

3. Next, stir in the multi-purpose flour, quick-cooking oats, baking soda, baking powder, salt, and cinnamon to the blender then blend until smooth and creamy.

4. Carefully divide the batter into the prepared muffin tins then sprinkle the diced chocolate on top.

5. Bake the muffins for 20 minutes or until a toothpick that is inserted into the muffins comes out clean then remove them from the oven.

6. Let the muffins rest in the muffin tins for 5 minutes then take them out of the muffin tins.

7. Transfer the muffins to a cooling rack. Then, let them cool.

8. Serve and enjoy.

## Coconut Carrot Muffins with Raisins

This is another vegetable muffin that is very recommended to try. With grated coconut and carrot, this muffin gives a crunchy sensation in every single bite. If you want it to be more coconut taste, you can replace half of the multipurpose flour with coconut flour. To enhance the taste and appearance, you can also give dust of powdered sugar on top. Besides, you can also glaze the muffin with melted chocolate, then sprinkle toasted coconut crumbles on top. Enjoy!

**Yield:** 10-12 muffins

**Cooking time:** 30 minutes

**Ingredients:**

- 1½ teaspoons ground cinnamon
- 1 teaspoon baking soda
- 1½ cups multi-purpose flour
- ¼ teaspoon salt
- ¼ cup granulated sugar
- ½ cup brown sugar
- 2 eggs
- ¾ cup vegetable oil
- 1 teaspoon vanilla
- 1 cup shredded carrots

- 3 tablespoons shredded coconut
- ¾ cup raisins

**Instructions:**

1. First, preheat an oven to 350°F (177°C) and prepare 12 muffin tins. Put a paper cup into each muffin tin then set aside.

2. Combine the multi-purpose flour with baking soda, ground cinnamon, and salt then mix well. Set aside.

3. In another bowl, whisk the brown sugar and granulated sugar with eggs then mix until smooth.

4. Add vanilla extract and vegetable oil to the egg mixture then stir until incorporated.

5. Pour the wet mixture into the dry mixture then mix until smooth.

6. After that, add shredded carrots and coconut to the batter then fold until combined.

7. Stir in the raisins to the batter then mix well.

8. Next, using an ice cream scoop, carefully divide the batter into the prepared muffin tins then inserts them into the preheated oven. Bake the muffins.

9. Once it is done, remove the muffins from the oven and let them rest for 5 minutes in the muffin tins.

10. Transfer the muffins to a cooling rack and let them cool.

11. Serve and enjoy.

## Healthy Spinach Greenies Muffins

It is the spinach that gives the beautiful green color to this muffin. Using raw honey as the sweetener agent, this muffin is surely kid-friendly. You can give it any names that will attract your kids' attention. Hulk muffin, Popeye muffin, Green muffin, and many other interesting names can be put for the muffin. For adult and older people, you can add a pinch of mint flavor to the muffin. It is surely amazing.

**Yield:** 10-12 muffins

**Cooking time:** 20 minutes

**Ingredients:**

- 1½ cups multi-purpose flour
- ½ cup applesauce
- 1 teaspoon baking powder
- 1 teaspoon vanilla extract
- ¼ teaspoon salt
- 2 eggs
- 1½ cups chopped baby spinach
- ¼ cup honey
- 2 tablespoons canola oil

- ¼ cup Choco chips

**Instructions:**

1. First, preheat an oven to 350°F (177°C) and prepare 12 muffin tins. Put a paper cup into each muffin tin then set aside.

2. Mix the multi-purpose flour with baking powder and salt then stir well. Sift the mixture and set aside.

3. Next, place applesauce, eggs, vanilla extract, baby spinach, sugar, and canola oil in a blender then blend until smooth.

4. Pour the spinach mixture into the dry mixture then fold to combine.

5. Divide the batter into the prepared muffin tins then sprinkle Choco chips on top.

6. Bake the muffins until a toothpick inserted into the muffins comes out clean.

7. Once it is done, remove the muffins from the oven and let them rest in the muffin tins for 5 minutes.

8. Take the muffins out of the tins then let them cool on a cooling rack.

9. Serve and enjoy.

**Brown Sugar Pumpkin Muffins with Walnuts Topping**

Pumpkin, chocolate, and nuts, what could be more awesome? The chocolate glaze and walnut crumble indeed make this muffin special. However, if accidentally chocolate and walnuts are not available, you can top the muffin with other delicious toppings, as you desire. Buttercream or cheese frosting with toasted coconut flakes, chocolate sprinkles, dried fruits, or candies could be the option. All of them will fit the muffin because the muffin itself is already delicious.

**Yield:** 10-12 muffins

**Cooking time:** 35 minutes

**Ingredients:**

- 1¼ cups multi-purpose flour
- 1 cup brown sugar
- 1 teaspoon baking soda
- ¾ teaspoon ground cinnamon
- ¼ teaspoon salt
- A pinch of nutmeg
- 1 egg
- ¾ cup canned pumpkin
- ¼ cup vegetable oil

**Topping:**

- ½ cup semi-sweet Choco chips
- ½ cup heavy cream
- ½ cup roasted walnuts crumble

**Instructions:**

1. First, preheat an oven to 350°F (177°C) and prepare 12 muffin tins. Put a paper cup into each muffin tin then set aside.

2. Combine the multi-purpose flour with brown sugar,

baking soda, ground cinnamon, salt, and nutmeg then mix well.

3. Whisk the egg with canned pumpkin and vegetable oil then stir until incorporated.

4. Gradually mix the wet mixture with the dry mixture then fold to combine.

5. Next, divide the batter into the prepared muffin tins then insert them into the preheated oven and bake the muffins for 25 minutes.

6. Once a toothpick inserted into the muffins comes out clean, remove the muffins from the oven and let them rest in the muffin tins for approximately 5 to 10 minutes.

7. Take the muffins out of the tins then arrange them on a cooling rack.

8. Next, melt the Choco chips together with heavy cream then stir until incorporated.

9. Let the chocolate mixture rest for a few minutes then baste it over the muffins.

10. Sprinkle roasted walnuts crumble on top then serve.

11. Enjoy!

## Savory Bok Choi Muffins with Sweet Corn

Not all people like to see vegetables in a muffin. However, this muffin is an exception. This muffin indeed performs a colorful yet beautiful muffin that will increase your appetite. Offering the nutritious content of the vegetables, the muffin is surely a great choice for everyone who cares about their healthy body and metabolism. Not to mention, the absence of sugar is a plus. For a vegan option, you can substitute the eggs with flax seeds.

**Yield:** 10-12 muffins

**Cooking time:** 30 minutes

**Ingredients:**

- 1½ cups multi-purpose flour
- 1 teaspoon baking powder
- ¼ teaspoon salt
- ¼ teaspoon pepper
- 2 eggs
- ½ cup plain yogurt
- ¼ cup olive oil
- ¼ cup sliced Bok Choi
- ½ cup sweet corn kernels

**Instructions:**

1. Preheat an oven to 400°F (204°C) and prepare 12 muffin tins. Put a paper tin into each muffin tin then set aside.

2. Add salt, pepper, and baking powder to the multi-purpose flour then mix well. Set aside.

3. In another bowl, whisk the eggs together with plain yogurt and olive oil until incorporated then pour the wet mixture into the dry mixture.

4. Stir in the sliced broccoli and corn kernels to the batter then mix until just combined.

5. Using an ice cream scoop divide the batter into the prepared muffin tins then insert them into the preheated oven and bake the muffin for 20 minutes.

6. Insert a toothpick into the muffins to check doneness and once it is done, remove the muffins from the oven.

7. Take the muffins out of the tins and transfer them to a serving dish.

8. Serve and enjoy.

**Whole Wheat Banana Palm Muffins**

This muffin is loaded with nutritious content that is good to start your active morning. The banana and whole wheat will fill you up until lunchtime; provide enough energy for you to face the busy day. Very ripe bananas are recommended for this recipe since they will be mashed easily, saving your time and energy. For an extra special touch, besides chocolate, you can put a dried banana chip on top.

**Yield:** 10-12 muffins

**Cooking time:** 30 minutes

**Ingredients:**

- ½ cup palm sugar
- 1 cup whole-wheat flour

- 1 cup cake flour
- 2 teaspoons baking powder
- ½ teaspoon cinnamon
- ¼ teaspoon salt
- 2 eggs
- 6 ripe bananas
- ½ cup butter
- ½ cup chopped dark chocolate compound

**Instructions:**

1. First, melt the butter over low heat. Then set aside.

2. Peel and mash the ripe bananas then set aside.

3. Preheat an oven to 350°F (177°C) and prepare 12 muffin tins. Put a paper cup into each muffin tin and set aside.

4. Mix the whole-wheat flour with the cake flour then add baking powder, salt, and cinnamon to the flour. Stir until combined.

5. In another bowl, place the palm sugar together with eggs then whisk until incorporated.

6. Add mashed banana and melted butter to the egg and palm sugar mixture then mix well.

7. Pour the wet mixture into the dry mixture until it is completely combined then divide the batter into the prepared muffin tins.

8. Next, sprinkle chopped dark chocolate on top of the muffins then bake them for 15 to 20 minutes.

9. Once it is done, remove the banana muffins from the oven and let them cool for approximately 5 minutes in the muffin tins. Transfer the muffins to a cooling rack.

10. Serve and enjoy.

## Shredded Carrots Sweet Whole Wheat Muffins

Filled with healthy ingredients and aromatic spices, this muffin is another perfect creation to start your busy morning. It contains whole-wheat flour, oats, and carrot that provide you enough energy throughout the day. Talking about the carrot, it is suggested to use baby carrots since they perform a wet but crunchy texture. Also, you are recommended to shred the carrot so that it can be easily blended with the batter. Cinnamon, ginger, and nutmeg are totally optional, but I keep using them for an extra flavor.

**Yield:** 10-12 muffins

**Cooking time:** 30 minutes

**Ingredients:**

- 1¼ cups whole-wheat flour
- 1 teaspoon baking powder
- ¼ teaspoon baking soda
- ¾ teaspoon ground cinnamon
- ½ teaspoon ginger
- A pinch of ground nutmeg
- 1½ cups shredded carrots
- ½ cup quick-cooking oats
- ¼ cup olive oil

- ½ cup honey
- 1 egg
- ¾ cup plain yogurt

**Instructions:**

1. First, preheat an oven to 425°F (218°C) and prepare 12 muffin tins. Put a paper cup into each muffin tin and set aside.

2. Combine the whole-wheat flour with baking powder, baking soda, ground cinnamon, ginger, and nutmeg. Mix well.

3. In another bowl, whisk the egg with olive oil, honey, and plain yogurt then pour the wet mixture into the dry mixture.

4. Next, add the quick-cooking oats with shredded carrots to the batter then fold until combined.

5. Using an ice cream scoop, carefully divide the batter into the prepared muffin tins then insert them into the preheated oven and bake the muffins.

6. Once it is done, remove the muffins from the oven and let them rest in the muffin tins for 5 minutes.

7. Take the muffins out of the tins then let them cool on a cooling rack.

8. Serve and enjoy.

## Flaxseed Meal Barley Muffins with Blueberries

Barley is a kind of whole grain that is rich in vitamins, minerals, fiber, and antioxidants. Along with flax seed that also has a bunch of health benefits, this muffin is perfect for any age, from toddler, adult, to the elderly. If you want another different taste, you can replace the blueberries with other fruits, chocolate chips, or nuts. Besides that, the muffin will look more tempting if you add some toppings on it. Cheese frosting seems to be a great idea.

**Yield:** 10-12 muffins

**Cooking time:** 30 minutes

**Ingredients:**

- 1½ cups barley flour
- 1 teaspoon baking powder
- ½ teaspoon ground cinnamon
- A pinch of salt
- 1½ tablespoons ground flaxseed meal
- ½ cup granulated sugar
- 2 eggs
- ¾ cup unsweetened almond milk
- 3 tablespoons olive oil

• 1 cup frozen blueberries

**Instructions:**

1. First, preheat an oven to 400°F (204°C) and prepare 12 muffin tins. Put a paper cup into each muffin tin and set aside.

2. Combine the barley flour with baking powder, cinnamon, salt, flaxseed meal, and granulated sugar in a bowl then mix well.

3. In another bowl, whisk eggs with almond milk and olive oil until incorporated then mix it with the dry mixture.

4. Next, add frozen blueberries to the batter then fold to combine.

5. Using an ice cream scoop divide the batter into the prepared muffin tins then insert them into the preheated oven and bake the muffins.

6. After 20 minutes, check the muffins and once it is done, remove them from the oven and let them rest in the muffin tins for 5 minutes.

7. Take the muffins out of the tins then arrange them on a cooling rack.

8. Serve and enjoy.


## Cassava Muffins with Sesame Seeds on Top

This muffin performs a heavy but soft muffin. It uses mashed cassava as the main ingredient. As well as mashed cassava, mashed potato, or mashed sweet potato will give the same result. With less amount of sugar, this muffin offers a not-very-sweet muffin that is surely perfect for those who decide to reduce sugar consumption. Dried raisins and chopped walnuts will be the best additional ingredients for the muffin.

**Yield:** 10-12 muffins

**Cooking time:** 50 minutes

**Ingredients:**

- ½ lb. cassava
- 3 eggs
- ¼ cup granulated sugar
- 2 tablespoons multi-purpose flour
- ¼ teaspoon baking soda
- ½ teaspoon baking powder
- ¼ cup butter
- 2 tablespoons sesame seeds

**Instructions:**

1. Peel the cassava then steam it until tender. Mash it until smooth.

2. Melt the butter over low heat then let it cool.

3. Preheat an oven to 350°F (177°C) and prepare 12 muffin tins. Put a paper cup into each muffin tin and set aside.

4. Combine the multi-purpose flour with baking soda and baking powder then set aside.

5. Whisk the sugar with eggs until fluffy then add the flour mixture to it. Mix well.

6. Stir in the mashed cassava to the batter then using a spatula fold it until combined.

7. Using an ice cream scoop divide the batter into the prepared muffin tins then sprinkle sesame seeds on top.

8. Insert the muffins into the preheated oven and bake them for 40 minutes.

9. Once it is done, remove the muffins from the oven and let them rest for approximately 5 minutes in the tins.

10. Take the muffins out of the tins and let them cool on a cooling rack.

11. Serve and enjoy.

## Savory Bacon Muffins with Coriander

This is a short-cut muffin recipe. It is simplified to help those who want to enjoy this nutritious muffin without spending so much time. It tastes good, though. However, if you want it to be more delicious, it is recommended to sauté the bacon with onion and season it with some spices before adding the bacon to the muffin batter. Besides, you can also add cheese to enhance the taste.

**Yield:** 10-12 muffins

**Cooking time:** 30 minutes

**Ingredients:**
- 1½ cups self-raising flour
- 3 tablespoons vegetable oil
- ¼ cup fresh milk
- 1 teaspoon ground coriander
- 1 teaspoon garlic powder
- 1 teaspoon onion powder
- 1 teaspoon chicken powder
- 3 eggs
- ½ cup diced bacon

**Instructions:**

1. Preheat an oven to 325°F (191°C) and prepare 12 muffin tins. Put a paper cup into each muffin tin and set aside.

2. Combine the vegetable oil with fresh milk then season the mixture with coriander, garlic powder, onion powder, and chicken powder. Stir until dissolved.

3. Add the eggs to the liquid mixture then whisk until smooth.

4. Pour the wet mixture into the flour then stir until incorporated.

5. Stir in the diced bacon to the batter then fold to combine.

6. Using a soup ladle fill the prepared muffin tins into ¾ full then insert them into the preheated oven and bake the muffins.

7. Once it is done or a toothpick inserted into the muffins comes out clean, remove the muffins from the oven and let them cool.

8. Serve and enjoy.

# Aromatic Clove Honey Muffins

Everyone will love this honey muffin! It is fluffy and light that will melt well in your mouth. With a little touch of vegetable oil, you will find that the muffin is very easy to swallow. In place of honey, you can also try agave. It can be a good replacement when honey is not available. Don't forget about the clove aroma along with cinnamon and allspice that will surely increase your appetite.

**Yield:** 10-12 muffins

**Cooking time:** 30 minutes

**Ingredients:**

- 1½ cups multi-purpose flour
- 1 teaspoon baking soda
- ¼ teaspoon salt
- ½ teaspoon ground cinnamon
- A pinch of ground cloves
- ¼ teaspoon allspice
- 3 tablespoons vegetable oil
- ¼ cup honey
- 1 egg

**Instructions:**

1. First, preheat an oven to 350°F (177°C) and prepare 12

muffin tins. Put a paper cup into each muffin tin and set aside.

2. Add salt, baking soda, ground cinnamon, ground cloves, and allspice to the multi-purpose flour then mix well. Sift the mixture.

3. In another bowl, mix vegetable oil with honey and egg then stir until incorporated.

4. Next, gradually pour the wet mixture into the dry mixture then stir until incorporated.

5. Using a soup ladle fill the prepared muffin tins into ¾ full then insert then into the preheated oven and bake the muffins for 12 to 15 minutes or until a toothpick inserted deeply into them comes out clean.

6. Once it is done, carefully remove the muffins from the oven and let them rest in the muffin tins for 5 minutes.

7. Take the muffins out of the tins then arrange them on a cooling rack.

8. Serve and enjoy.


## Turmeric Yellow Muffins with Herb Streusels

This muffin is loaded with flavorful spices and healthy sweeteners. Using raw honey and maple syrup, this muffin performs a natural sweetness that is good for your body.

Because the muffin uses lots of egg, it will have a little bit of cake texture, which is soft and fluffy. If you want your muffin to taste heavier, you can remove one or two eggs from this recipe. Another delicious thing of this muffin is the spiced streusel topping that is so crumbing and mouthwatering.

**Yield:** 10-12 muffins

**Cooking time:** 35 minutes

**Ingredients:**

- 5 eggs
- ¾ cup unsweetened almond milk
- ¼ cup maple syrup
- 2 tablespoons honey
- 2 teaspoons almond extract
- 1 cup coconut flour
- 1½ teaspoons ground turmeric
- ¼ teaspoon ground ginger
- ¾ teaspoon baking soda
- ¼ teaspoon salt

**Topping:**

- ½ cup brown sugar
- 2 tablespoons multi-purpose flour
- 2 teaspoons ground cinnamon
- A pinch of ground cloves
- A pinch of ground nutmeg
- ¼ cup pecan crumbles
- 3 tablespoons butter

**Instructions:**

1. Mix the brown sugar with multi-purpose flour, cinnamon, cloves, nutmeg, and pecan crumbles then stir until combined.

2. Cut the butter into small cubes then add them to the brown sugar mixture. Using your fingers combine the streusels mixture until becoming crumbles.

3. Preheat an oven to 350°F (177°C) and prepare 12 muffin tins. Put a paper cup into each muffin tin and set aside.

4. Combine the coconut flour with turmeric, ginger, salt, and baking soda. Mix well and sift the flour.

5. Crack the eggs then place them in a bowl. Whisk until incorporated.

6. Add almond milk, maple syrup, honey, and almond extract to the eggs then whisk until combined.

7. After that, stir in the dry mixture to the wet mixture then mix well.

8. Divide the batter into the prepared muffin tins then sprinkle the streusels on top.

9. Insert the muffins into the preheated oven and bake them for 25 minutes or until a toothpick inserted into the muffins comes out clean.

10. Once it is done, remove the muffins from the oven but let them rest in the muffin tins for 5 minutes.

11. After 5 minutes, take the muffins out of the muffin tins then arrange them on a cooling rack.

12. Serve and enjoy.

# Dairy Free Turmeric Ginger Muffins with Aniseed

Though this muffin is dairy-free, you don't need to worry about it being dry. The coconut milk and vegetable oil used in this recipe surely do their job very well, resulting in a moist, soft, and fluffy muffin. Served with several spices, this muffin also offers an aromatic muffin that will increase your appetite. Not to mention, the aniseeds that are included in the muffin. They are actually rich in nutrients, which are good for body health.

**Yield:** 10-12 muffins

**Cooking time:** 35 minutes

**Ingredients:**

- 1 cup multi-purpose flour
- 1½ teaspoons baking powder
- ¼ teaspoon salt
- 2 tablespoons granulated sugar
- 1 egg
- 2 teaspoons ground turmeric
- 1 teaspoon pumpkin pie spice
- ½ teaspoon grated ginger
- ¾ cup coconut milk
- ½ cup vegetable oil

- ½ cup honey
- 1 teaspoon aniseeds

**Instructions:**

1. First, preheat an oven to 375°F and prepare 12 muffin tins. Line each muffin tin with a paper cup then set aside.

2. Add salt and baking powder to the multi-purpose flour then mix well.

3. In another bowl, combine the granulated sugar with the egg then whisk until incorporated.

4. Next, season the egg mixture with turmeric, pumpkin pie spice, and grated ginger then pour coconut milk, vegetable oil, and honey into it. Mix well.

5. Pour the wet mixture over the dry mixture then whisk until combined.

6. Add aniseeds to the batter then fold to mix.

7. Using an ice cream scoop or a soup ladle, divide the batter into the prepared muffin tins. Then, bake them for approximately 20 minutes or until a toothpick inserted into them comes out clean.

8. Then, let the muffins rest for 5 minutes in the muffin tins and transfer them to a cooling rack.

9. Serve and enjoy.

# Dairy-Free Applesauce Sweet Muffins

Another dairy-free option, this muffin is a good choice to be put into your kid's lunch box. The applesauce used in this recipe is not only healthy but also moist and delicious. To enhance the taste and aroma, you can add ground cinnamon to the recipe. If your kids don't have any nut allergies, you can also add some chopped almond, pecans, walnuts, and other nuts for topping.

**Yield:** 10-12 muffins

**Cooking time:** 35 minutes

**Ingredients:**

- 1½ cups multi-purpose flour
- ½ cup granulated sugar
- 1 teaspoon baking powder
- ¼ teaspoon salt
- ½ cup applesauce
- 2 tablespoons unsweetened almond milk
- 1 tablespoon white vinegar
- ½ cup coconut milk

**Instructions:**

1. First, preheat an oven to 400°F (204°C) and prepare 12 muffin tins. Line each muffin tin with a paper cup then set aside.

2. Combine the multi-purpose flour with granulated sugar, baking powder, and salt then mix well.

3. Next, whisk the applesauce together with white vinegar, coconut milk, and almond milk until incorporated then pour it into the dry mixture. Fold until combined.

4. Using a soup ladle divide the batter into the prepared muffin tins then insert them into the preheated oven and bake the muffins for 20-25minutes.

5. Once it is done, or when a toothpick inserted into the muffins comes out clean, carefully remove the muffins from the oven.

6. Let the muffins rest in the tins for 5 minutes before taking them out of the tins then transfer the muffins to a cooling rack.

7. Serve and enjoy.

# CONCLUSION

Thank you for having this book!

Now you are undoubtedly on the last page of the book.

I do expect this book can be a great partner in your kitchen to prepare the tastiest and the healthiest muffins for your beloved ones. I also hope that this book is able to answer all your questions about muffin making.

Please note that practices make perfect. That is why I strongly suggest you make the muffins as often as possible.

Pick your own favorite recipes and bake them in your lovely kitchen. Serve only the most delicious and scrumptious muffins from your home.

Happy baking, good people!

CPSIA information can be obtained
at www.ICGtesting.com
Printed in the USA
LVHW081021270222
712135LV00012B/624